Associate Editor: Malcolm Page

File on
O'NEILL

Compiled by Stephen A. Black

Methuen Drama

A Methuen Drama Book
First published in 1993 as a paperback original
by Methuen Drama, Michelin House,
81 Fulham Road, London SW3 6RB,
and HEB Inc., 361 Hanover Street,
Portsmouth, New Hampshire 03801-3959, USA

Front cover photograph of Eugene O'Neill
copyright © The Hulton-Deutsch Collection

Typeset in 9/10 Times by
L. Anderson Typesetting,
Woodchurch, Kent TN26 3TB

Printed in Great Britain

ISBN 0 413 66330 2

British Library Cataloguing in Publication Data
is available from the British Library

Contents

Acknowledgements

The compiler is grateful to Yale University Press, as legatee under
the will of Carlotta Monterey O'Neill, and to the Collection of
American Literature, Beinecke Rare Book and Manuscript Library,
Yale University, for permission to quote from selected letters, articles,
and other writings by Eugene O'Neill.

My thanks are also due to Malcolm Page, who shared with me his
file of theatrical reviews, his expertise in British theatrical lore, and
his advice concerning this book.

The theatre is, by its nature, an ephemeral art: yet it is a daunting task to track down the newspaper reviews, or contemporary statements from the writer or his director, which are often all that remain to help us recreate some sense of what a particular production was like. This series is therefore intended to make readily available a selection of the comments that the critics made about the plays of leading modern dramatists at the time of their production — and to trace, too, the course of each writer's own views about his work and his world.

In addition to combining a uniquely convenient source of such elusive *documentation*, the 'Writer-Files' series also assembles the *information* necessary for readers to pursue further their interest in a particular writer or work. Variations in quantity between one writer's output and another's, differences in temperament which make some readier than others to talk about their work, and the variety of critical response, all mean that the presentation and balance of material shifts between one volume and another: but we have tried to arrive at a format for the series which will nevertheless enable users of one volume readily to find their way around any other.

Section 1, 'A Brief Chronology', provides a quick conspective overview of each playwright's life and career. *Section 2* deals with the plays themselves, arranged chronologically in the order of their composition: information on first performances, major revivals, and publication is followed by a brief synopsis (for quick reference set in slightly larger, italic type), then by a representative selection of the critical response, and of the dramatist's own comments on the play and its theme.

Section 3 offers concise guidance to each writer's work in non-dramatic forms, while *Section 4*, 'The Writer on His Work', brings together comments from the playwright himself on more general matters of construction, opinion, and artistic development. Finally, *Section 5* provides a bibliographical guide to other primary and secondary sources of further reading, among which full details will be found of works cited elsewhere under short titles, and of collected editions of the plays — but not of individual titles, particulars of which will be found with the other factual data in Section 2.

The 'Writer-Files' hope by striking this kind of balance between information and a wide range of opinion to offer 'companions' to the study of major playwrights in the modern repertoire — not in that dangerous pre-digested fashion which

General Editor's Introduction

5

can too readily quench the desire to read the plays themselves, nor so prescriptively as to allow any single line of approach to predominate, but rather to encourage readers to form their own judgements of the plays in a wide-ranging context.

Eugene O'Neill may have lacked certain qualities thought desirable in a dramatist — chronically a sense of proportion, occasionally a sense of humour. Yet single-handedly he created a distinctively American drama, while also drawing fruitfully upon both European traditionalism and European modernism. As early as *The Emperor Jones* and *The Hairy Ape* he was thus trying his own variations on the expressionist mode, while his continuing fascination with classical theatre led to experiments with masks, pantomime, and the use of a chorus, finding its greatest fulfilment in *Mourning Becomes Electra*.

Yet if O'Neill's career finally described a full circle back to its naturalistic origins, the psychological depths of the later plays, which both embrace and transcend personal despair, lend them a quality that is different in kind from the early works, deeply though these drew upon the lore and language of the sea. The sense of fatalism which was perhaps what he found most sympathetic in Greek tragedy thus came to blend aptly enough with the social determinism in which *The Iceman Cometh* was so profoundly steeped.

Restored now to honour as a prophet in his own country, in his later years O'Neill was perhaps more fully appreciated in Europe — notably in Scandinavia, from whence he seems to have absorbed the very different obsessions of Ibsen and Strindberg. With Ibsen, he sought for symbols through which to express the universal and allusive in what the theatre made immediate and explicit. With Strindberg, he fused his personal and family life into his art at almost every point — a compulsion finally and triumphantly purged in *Long Day's Journey into Night*. Yet it was with other writers of his own nation that he shared a striving for sheer scale — whether challenging an audience's endurance with nine acts instead of three, or planning his own epic portrayal of America, betrayed by its own materialism and greed, in a cycle of up to eleven plays, of which only *A Touch of the Poet* was to survive in a final form.

The sweep of O'Neill's achievement was, then, challenged by the scale of his own ambitions. If, as some critics argue, his sensibility was also limited by a lack of self-knowledge, that lack was probably inseparable from the discontent which drove him — destructively as a man, but creatively as an artist. As recorded on page 91, he came to believe that the United States, 'instead of being the most successful country in the world, is the greatest failure': if, we may feel, that failure was always inseparable from the greatness, so also was his own.

Simon Trussler

1888 16 Oct., Eugene Gladstone O'Neill born in New York, third son of James O'Neill, a prominent actor, and Mary Ellen Quinlan (known as Ella). The first son, James Jr. (Jamie or Jim) is ten years older; the second son, Edmund, dies, aged about 18 months, in Mar. 1885, having caught measles from Jamie. Eugene's birth being difficult, a doctor prescribes morphine for Ella, to which she is addicted until 1914.

1888-95 O'Neill is raised mainly by a nanny, who remains with him until he is seven. The family travels the country ten months of the year, his father acting in the melodrama he owns, *The Count of Monte Cristo*. They summer in a seaside cottage in New London, Connecticut.

1895 Enrols in boarding school at Riverdale, New York, where Jamie begins first year at St. John's College (later Fordham University).

1902 Having earlier rejected Catholicism, he persuades his father to send him to the secular Betts Academy, in Stamford, Connecticut.

1903 Late summer, learns of mother's morphine addiction, and that it began with his birth. Begins to drink heavily and rebels against his father. Reads widely in 'advanced' authors.

1906-09 Graduates from Betts with a good record and is admitted to Princeton, which drops him during his second semester for missing too many classes. Father gets him a secretarial job and supplements his salary with an allowance. He reads Nietzsche, Ibsen, Schopenhauer, Wilde, Swinburne, Whitman, Melville, Yeats, and writes wretched poetry in imitation of Rossetti and Dowson, becoming friendly with Greenwich Village artists and radicals.

1909 Affair with Kathleen Jenkins. When she becomes pregnant they plan to marry, but Eugene also tells his father he feels he is being trapped into marriage. 2 Oct., they secretly marry, a day or so before Eugene sails for Honduras on a gold-prospecting venture his father has arranged to help his son avoid marriage.

1910 10 May, Eugene Gladstone O'Neill II is born. O'Neill, home from Honduras with malaria, apparently sees his son briefly before sailing for Buenos Aires where he lives down and out until the following April.

1911 Steams to Liverpool as a common sailor, returning to New York rated 'Able Bodied Seaman'. Lives in waterfront flophouse.

1912 Jan., when Kathleen Jenkins files for divorce, guilt leads Eugene to nearly successful suicide attempt. Nov., tuberculosis diagnosed, and enters sanatorium on Christmas Day.

1913 Starts writing plays. June, discharged from sanitorium.

1914 Ella O'Neill becomes permanently free from morphine addiction. James O'Neill arranges subsidized publication of *Thirst and Other One Act Plays* (including *The Web*, *Warnings*, *Fog*, and *Recklessness*). Eugene enrolls as special student at Harvard for G. P. Baker's play-writing course.

1916 28 July, first performance of an O'Neill play, *Bound East for Cardiff*, in Provincetown, Massachusetts. He has now written at least 20 plays. Meets Saxe Commins, a would-be playwright, later O'Neill's dentist, then his editor and lifelong friend. Love affair with Louise Bryant.

1918 Has now written more than thirty plays. 12 Apr., marries Agnes Boulton. Writes first major play, *Beyond the Horizon*.

1919 Meets George Jean Nathan, lifelong friend. 30 Oct., birth of Shane Rudraighe O'Neill. *The Dreamy Kid* performed with black cast.

1920 Feb., *Beyond the Horizon* produced, and wins admiration of O'Neill's father as well as critics and public. Father suffers stroke ten days after the opening, and intestinal cancer is later diagnosed. June, Pulitzer Prize awarded to *Beyond the Horizon*. Father dies in August, aged 74. O'Neill revises *Chris Christopherson* into *Anna Christie*, and writes *The Emperor Jones* and *Diff'rent*.

1921 Meets son, Eugene Jr., for first time since infancy; they remain close for the rest of the son's life. Writes *Gold*, drafts *The First Man* and *The Fountain*. Meets Kenneth Macgowan and Robert Edmond Jones, director and designer for several O'Neill productions. Nov., *Anna Christie* and *The Straw* open. Dec., writes *The Hairy Ape* in three weeks.

1922 O'Neill's mother goes into coma in Los Angeles, and dies of brain tumour, 28 Feb., her body reaching New York on the same evening *The Hairy Ape* opens. *Anna Christie* wins Pulitzer Prize.

1923 Gold medal from National Institute of Arts and Letters. *Anna Christie* opens successful run in London. Completes *Welded*, begins *Marco Millions* and *All God's Chillun Got Wings*. Older brother Jamie, sober since his father died, deliberately begins to drink himself to death when mother stricken, and in June committed to asylum in alcoholic psychosis; dies 8 Nov.

1924 Writes *Desire under the Elms*. Production of *All God's Chillun* with Paul Robeson threatened by Ku Klux Klan, but eventually has successful run. *Welded* closes after 24 performances. O'Neill's arrangement of *The Ancient Mariner* plays 33 performances at the Province-town Playhouse. 11 Nov., opening of *Desire*.

1925 *Desire* threatened with prosecution for 'indecency', but has New York run of 208 performances; banned in Boston and England. 14 May, Oona born in Bermuda. Completes *Great God Brown*. O'Neill drinks heavily all year, contemplates psychotherapy to stop.

1926 Stops drinking at New Year, and has six weeks of treatment with a New York analyst. Begins *Strange Interlude*. Marriage with Agnes Boulton deteriorates. Meets actress Carlotta Monterey; their affair probably begins in the autumn.

1927 Apr., *Marco Millions* published. Nov., *Lazarus Laughed* published. *Marco Millions* and *Strange Interlude* optioned by Theatre Guild. Suffers ill health and depression. Eugene Jr. enters Yale University to study classics.

1928 Feb., elopes with Carlotta to France, remains until 1931. Writes *Dynamo*. Bitter quarrels with Agnes via press. Pasadena Playhouse performs *Lazarus*. *Strange Interlude* awarded Pulitzer Prize. 5 Oct., Eugene and Carlotta sail for Far East, stopping in Saigon, Shanghai, Manila, and Singapore.

1929 After quarrels and drinking bouts, Carlotta leaves O'Neill in Colombo, but is reunited in Port Said. They rent villa on Riviera. *Dynamo* opens, to severe reviews: revises text for publication. Suit by woman who claims O'Neill plagiarized *Interlude*; suit dismissed in 1931 as 'wholly preposterous'. Agnes granted divorce in Reno on grounds of desertion. 22 July, O'Neill and Carlotta marry. O'Neill buys a Mercedes, then a Bugatti, then a Renault. Begins *Mourning Becomes Electra*.

1930 Completes four drafts of *Electra*. Sees Kamerny Theatre of Moscow perform *All God's Chillun* and *Desire*.

1931 Completes fifth and sixth drafts of *Electra* by 27 March, and sends manuscript to Theatre Guild. Returns to US for *Electra* rehearsals, and is met by Nathan and Eugene Jr. 16 June, Eugene Jr. marries Elizabeth Greene. 26 Oct., *Electra* highly acclaimed, begins successful run. Shane enters Lawrenceville School.

1932 O'Neills build house at Sea Island, Georgia. Meets Carlotta's mother and daughter (from second marriage); visits from Saxe and Dorothy Commins, Shane and Oona, Writes three drafts of only 'Catholic' play, *Days without End*, intended as part of unfinished trilogy. Writes *Ah, Wilderness!* in four weeks in September.

1933 7 Jan., *Emperor Jones* opens as opera at the Metropolitan, and as film with Paul Robeson. Boni and Liveright, publishers of O'Neill, Faulkner, Hemingway, Hart Crane, and others, collapses; Saxe Commins secures royalties owed to O'Neill before the end. Bennett Cerf buys Modern Library from Boni, founds Random House. O'Neill agrees to contract with Random if Saxe hired as editor. 25 Sept., *Ah, Wilderness!* opens, and begins long run. Finishes seventh draft *Days without End* just before Theatre Guild begins rehearsals.

1934 8 Jan., *Days without End* opens to unfavorable reviews, except from Catholic critics, and is last new O'Neill play produced until 1946. O'Neill warned by doctors to rest or risk a general breakdown.

1935 Begins planning the 'Cycle', on which he works continuously until June, 1939, never finished. The Cycle, eventually a series of eleven plays, outlines theory of American history from the 1790s to 1930. Works on *A Touch of the Poet*. Sick and depressed. Shane disappears briefly while on vacation from the Florida military school he now attends.

1936 When health problems continue, O'Neill decides to leave Georgia, visits friend in Seattle, rents a house overlooking Puget Sound, where on 12 Nov. he is besieged by press at news that he has been awarded the Nobel Prize. Moves to San Francisco, hospitalized with abdominal symptoms. 29 Dec., appendectomy.

1937 Jan., almost dies from post-operative complications. Sea Island house sells at loss. The O'Neills buy 157-acre hilltop site east of San Francisco Bay, and build Tao House, moving in on 30 Dec. Health problems all year.

1938 Begins *More Stately Mansions*. Shane transfers to a school in Colorado, later deciding to return to Lawrenceville. Both O'Neills suffer health problems and depression. Eugene Jr. and Whitney Oates's two-volume *Complete Greek Drama* published by Random.

1939 Sick and depressed. 5 June, revising third play of 'Cycle', *A Touch of the Poet*, he notes: 'Feel fed up and stale on Cycle after four and a half years . . . will do me good lay on shelf and forget it for a while — do a play which has nothing to do with it'. Two days later has title, *The Iceman Cometh*, draws plans for set, and begins outline. When scenario finished, he begins scenario for another new play, 'The Long Day's Journey'. July, begins writing *Iceman,* finishing third draft in Dec.; begins trimming.

1940 With *Iceman* finished, thoughts turn to Cycle, and depression returns. Mar., begins *Long Day's Journey into Night*. May, work stops with the war news: 'Glued to radio', he writes in his diary, 'to hell with trying to work — it's too insignificant in this madmen's world'. Sept., completes first draft, and play essentially finished in Oct. O'Neill returns to Cycle and other new play ideas. Likes film *The Long Voyage Home*. Health deteriorates; a lifelong 'familial' tremor worsens.

1941 Apr., begins and finishes *Hughie*. Oct., begins *A Moon for the Misbegotten*, working on through the bombing of Pearl Harbour: 'War or not — the Archimedes viewpoint should be the artist's (as long as he is physically out, anyway — stick to one's job)'. Shane enlists in Merchant Marines.

1942 Jan., draft of *A Moon for the Misbegotten* finished. Health problems severe: tremor increasingly interferes with O'Neill's writing. Nov., finishes revising *A Touch of the Poet*. Quarrels with Oona, whom he thinks spoiled. Shane has nervous breakdown.

1943 Though physically almost unable to write, continues to get new play ideas at his usual fecund rate. Finishes *A Moon for the Misbegotten*, his last completed play. Tries to learn to compose by typing and dictating, but cannot change a lifelong process. 16 June, Oona marries Charlie Chaplin, and tries to reconcile with her father, but is rebuffed. Relations strained between O'Neills.

1944 O'Neills sell Tao House, move to a San Francisco hotel. Tremor now affecting his entire body making speech difficult.

1945 O'Neills move to New York. Their relationship deteriorates with mutual accusations of infidelity, and other problems. Eugene Jr., drinking heavily, loses his academic career. Sends sealed copy of *Long Day's Journey* to Cerf with instructions that the play is never to be performed, but may be published 25 years after his death.

1946 Works on Theatre Guild production of *Iceman*, but is too ill to correct the problems he sees in performance. Oct., opens to praise from reviewers.

1947 Theatre Guild tries out *A Moon* on tour, where it fails. Problems between O'Neills worsen.

1948 Carlotta leaves, O'Neill breaks arm in fall and considers divorce, reconciliation in March. Shane arrested for possession of heroin, O'Neill refusing to make his bail. O'Neills buy house by sea near Boston. O'Neill now almost completely incapacitated.

1950 25 Sept., Eugene Jr. kills himself.

1951 5 Feb., after quarrel with Carlotta, O'Neill falls in snow, breaks his leg, and nearly freezes to death. Carlotta hospitalized in a bromide psychosis. They contemplate permanent separation. O'Neill, weighing under 100 pounds, and also suffering from bromide poisoning, develops pneumonia. Reconciled with Carlotta in May. They move to Shelton Hotel, where O'Neill remains rest of his life.

1952 *A Moon for the Misbegotten* published by Random. Destroys many drafts and manuscripts.

1953 27 Nov., O'Neill dies. 2 Dec., buried privately at Forest Hills Cemetery, Boston.

1956 2 Feb., premiere of *Long Day's Journey Into Night* in Stockholm, and simultaneous publication of the play by Yale University Press, Bennett Cerf, in accordance with O'Neill's instructions, having declined to publish. 7 Nov., American premiere, which ran for 390 performances, and won O'Neill a fourth Pulitzer Prize.

A Wife for a Life

'A Play in One Act.'
Written: 1913.
First performed: Lotus Theatre Group, Playhouse 46, St.
    Clement's Church, New York, 4-20 Nov. 1982 (dir.
    Michael Fields).
Published: in *Lost Plays*; *Ten 'Lost' Plays*; *Complete Plays
    1913-1920.*

---

*Jack and 'Older Man' have found gold in Arizona. One
of them will have to go East to organize a company;
Jack wants to go because he loves a woman there. As
Jack talks of his love, the audience soon realizes the
woman is the older man's estranged wife. The rest of the
play is about the older man's reaction to his friend's
revelations. Jack eventually leaves with the older man's
blessings, still unaware they have been rivals.*

The Web

'A Play in One Act.'
Written: 1913.
First performed: Lotus Theatre Group, Playhouse 46, St.
    Clement's Church, New York, 4-20 Nov. 1982 (dir.
    Michael Fields).
Published: in *Thirst*; *Lost Plays*; *Ten 'Lost' Plays*; *Complete
    Plays 1913-1920.*

---

*The prostitute Rose has a consumptive cough and a
baby, both of which annoy her pimp, Steve. In their
quarrel Steve threatens to turn her in to the police
which will cause her child to be taken from her. Tim, an
escaped prisoner, hears them fight, and enters with a
gun to protect Rose. After Steve leaves threatening
revenge, Rose tells Tim her problems and he gives
hermoney. Steve shoots Tim through the window, drops
the gun in the room, and flees. Two policemen who have*

13

*been looking for Tim enter, find the gun, and arrest Rose for
killing and robbing Tim. The irony of the trap — the web —
fascinates Rose. In a stage direction O'Neill says of her: 'She
seems to be aware of something in the room which none of the
others can see — perhaps the personification of the ironic life
force that has crushed her.'*

[The title and German naturalist manner link the play to Hauptmann's
Die Weber (*The Weavers*), which O'Neill had probably recently read. In
1916 he saw the play six times. See Margaret Ranald, *The Eugene
O'Neill Companion*, p. 713.]

Thirst

'A Play in One Act.'
Written: 1913.
First performed: Wharf Th., Provincetown, Mass., Aug. 1916
 (dir. George Cram Cook, who played the Gentleman; with Louise
 Bryant as the Dancer and O'Neill as the West Indian Sailor).
Published: in *Thirst*; *Lost Plays*; *Ten 'Lost' Plays*; *Complete Plays
 1913-1920*.

*The three characters, dying of thirst in a lifeboat, watch shark
fins circle the boat. The Gentleman and Dancer fret about the
silence and ennui, while the sailor hums a charm to keep the
sharks away. All three become progressively more mad. Con-
vinced he is hiding the water they all need, the Dancer offers
herself to the sailor who spurns her. She begins to dance like a
'marionette', then collapses and dies. The sailor says that now
they can eat and drink — from her body. The gentleman pushes
her body into the sea where the sharks eat it. The sailor stabs the
gentleman but both fall overboard and the sharks eat again.*

Recklessness

'A Play in One Act.'
Written: 1913.

Unperformed on stage, *Recklessness* is the putative source for the film,
  The Constant Woman (Fox, 1933; dir. Victor Schertizinger).
Published: in *Thirst*; *Lost Plays*; *Ten 'Lost' Plays*; *Complete Plays
  1913-1920*.

---

*Mildred Baldwin, a bird in a gilded cage, loathes her husband,
Arthur, and loves the chauffeur, Fred. Discovering their affair,
Arthur tricks Fred into driving dangerously in a damaged car.
He soon learns that Fred has been killed. He accuses his wife but
seems to agree to let her go off with Fred. Fred's body is brought
into the house. Mildred faints, awakens, and goes upstairs to
shoot herself.*

Warnings

'A Play in One Act.'
Written: 1913.
Unperformed.
Published: in *Thirst*; *Ten 'Lost' Plays*; *Complete Plays 1913-1920*.

---

*James Knapp, a ship's wireless operator, is ashore when he
learns he is going deaf. He knows he should find other work, but
his wife complains about poverty and he agrees to go on one last
voyage. In Scene ii, his ship sinking, Knapp reveals his deafness
to his captain, and accepts blame for the collision. As lifeboats
evacuate the crew, Knapp shoots himself.*

Fog

'A Play in One Act.'
Written: 1914.
First performed: Playwrights' Th., New York, 5 Jan. 1917 (dir. O'Neill;
  with Hutchinson Collins, Margaret Swain, and Karl Karstens).
Published: in *Thirst*; *Lost Plays*; *Ten 'Lost' Plays*; *Complete Plays
  1913-1920*.

A Polish peasant woman and her dead child, a businessman, and a poet drift in a fogbound lifeboat off Newfoundland. The poet expounds 'humanism', and the businessman tries to be hopeful. When a steamer seems about to rescue them, they drift against an iceberg. The poet realizes that if they shout for help they may lure the steamer into collision with the berg. He and the businessman quarrel, the poet stifling the businessman's attempts to shout. Nevertheless, they soon hear a boat rowing toward them. The Officer tells them the child's crying led the rescuing rowboat directly to the lifeboat. Both men swear the child died the day before. The Officer thinks both are mad. One of the stronger of O'Neill's pre-1918 plays, Fog *shows the influence of Stephen Crane's* The Open Boat *in both situation and style.*

Bread and Butter

'A Play in Four Acts.'
Written: 1914.
Unperformed.
Published: in *Children of the Sea; Complete Plays 1913-1920.*

In Bridgeport, artistically promising John Brown loves the silly Maud. His father wants to send him to law school, but Maud's father believes he can succeed as a commercial artist. In New York John lives a bohemian life with other painters and works happily on impressionist nudes and landscapes. But when his father cuts off his allowance, he is forced to work on the docks, which destroys his desire to paint, and he starts drinking. His family and Maud visit to urge him to return to Bridgeport, marry, and take a job in his father-in-law's business. He reluctantly agrees. Two years later, drinking heavily and miserable in his marriage, he kills himself to escape Maud. The tone of a few lines is reminiscent of Long Day's Journey into Night.

Children of the Sea

'A Play in One Act.'

Written: 1914.
Unperformed in this version. See *Bound East for Cardiff.*
Published: in *The Provincetown Plays, First Series* (New York: Frank
   Shay, 1916); *Children of the Sea.*

Very important from my point of view. In it can be seen — or felt — the
germ of the spirit, life — attitude, etc., of all my more important future
work. And it was written practically within my first half-year as a
playwright, before I went to Baker, under whose influence the following
year I did nothing one-tenth as original.

> O'Neill, letter to Richard Dana Skinner, *c.* July 1934.

Bound East for Cardiff

'A Play in One Act.'
Written: copyright 1914 as *Children of the Sea*; revised 1916.
First performed: Wharf Th., Provincetown, Mass., 28 July 1916
   (dir. O'Neill; with George Cram Cook as Yank, Frederick Burt as
   Driscoll, E. J. Ballantyne as Cocky, Harry Kemp as Davis, O'Neill as
   the Second Mate, and John Reed and Wilbur Daniel Steele in small
   parts), trans. to Playwright's Th., New York, 3 Nov. 1916 (with
   largely same cast).
Revived: frequently, often with the other one act plays set on board the
   S.S. Glencairn, *The Long Voyage Home, In the Zone,* and *The Moon
   of the Caribees:* see under *The Long Voyage Home.*
Film and television: see under *The Long Voyage Home.*
Published: in *The Moon of the Caribees and Six Other Plays of the Sea*
   (Boni and Liveright, 1919); *Plays I*; *Complete Plays 1913-1920.*

A play which owes more to the creation of mood and atmosphere than to
any fundamentally interesting idea or sudden twist of plot. [It] merely
shows the death of a sailor in the forecastle of a British tramp on a foggy
night. The appeal lies in the successful approximation of true talk . . . .
Approximation, rather than faithful reproduction, must be the aim of the
dramatist who deals with the looser talking sort of folk. Obviously, it is
impossible to set down the conversation of sailors word for word. [When
O'Neill occasionally fails it is when] the spirit is false. Such slips are
few in the play. Eugene O'Neill . . . is probably familiar with the
subject.

> Heywood Broun, *New York Tribune*, 30 Jan. 1917

Abortion

'A Play in One Act.'
Written: 1914.
First performed: Key Th., St. Mark's Square, New York, 27 Oct. 1959.
Published: in *Thirst; Lost Plays; Ten 'Lost' Plays; Complete Plays 1913-1920.*

Jack Townsend, Princeton baseball hero, surrounded at homecoming by his 'swell' family and fiancee, has told his father he has made a 'town' girl pregnant. The father has helped him arrange an abortion, and both believe all is well. The girl's brother confronts Jack, accusing him of killing his sister and of being cowardly. Jack, stunned at the news, offers reparation but is spurned, and after they argue, shoots himself.

The play . . . [demonstrates] O'Neill's preoccupation with his responsibility for the pregnancy of Kathleen Jenkins who became his first wife and the mother of his son. . . .

Margaret Ranald, *Eugene O'Neill Companion,* p. 4.

The Movie Man

'A Comedy in One Act.'
Written: 1914.
First performed: Key Th., St. Mark's Square, New York, 27 Oct. 1959.
Revived: Lotus Theatre Group, Playhouse 46, St. Clement's Church, New York, 4-20 Nov. 1982 (dir. Michael Fields).
Published: in *Thirst; Lost Plays; Ten 'Lost' Plays; Complete Plays 1913-1920.*

Rogers, representing an American movie company filming a Mexican revolution, contracts with Pancho Gomez, the Mexican commander, to fight only when weather permits photography. A beautiful Mexican girl comes to plead with Gomez for the life of her father, a prisoner. Rogers wins the girl's favour by giving Gomez permission to make a surprise attack at night in return for the life of the girl's father.

[O'Neill planned to go with John Reed to cover Pancho Villa's Mexican revolution, but did not. See Gelb and Gelb, *O'Neill*, p. 262.]

Servitude

'A Play in Three Acts'.
Written: 1914.
First performed: Skylark Th., New York International Airport, New York, 22 Apr. 1960.
Revived: Univ. of Wisconsin Center, Richland, 14 Nov. 1981 (dir. Paul Voelker).
Published: in *Thirst*; *Lost Plays*; *Ten 'Lost' Plays*; *Complete Plays 1913-1920*.

Mrs. Frazer comes late one night to meet a famous novelist, David Roylston, whom she has loved for his writings. She has left her husband and is trying to find herself in the ways Roylston's novels recommend. He lets her spend the night in a guest room. In Act II Roylston's wife returns, finds Mrs. Frazer, assumes Roylston loves her, and is prepared to leave, feeling the time has come for her to atone for her sin of loving Roylston sexually before they married. The row between the three continues into Act III, and is further complicated by the entry of Mr. Frazer. The play ends with both couples reconciled, their understanding of their marriages enlarged by the revelations of the play.

This early well-made play is . . . in the manner of Ibsen and it tries to answer the question of what happened to Nora Helmer . . . after she slammed the door. . . . The dialogue has a Shavian quality [and develops] the theme of the superman, not so much in the Nietzschean sense, but rather that of Bernard Shaw.

Ranald, *Eugene O'Neill Companion*, p. 632.

The Sniper

'A Play in One Act.'
First performed: Playwright's Th., New York, 16 Feb. 1917 (dir. Nina Moise; with George Cram Cook, Donald Corley, and Theron Bamberger).

Revived: Key Th., St. Mark's Square., New York, 27 Oct. 1959.
Published: in *Thirst*; *Lost Plays*; *Ten 'Lost' Plays*; *Complete Plays 1913-1920.*

Rougon, a Belgian peasant, has just seen his soldier son killed in action near his ruined cottage. A priest tries to console Rougon, but when a boy brings the news that Rougon's wife and his dead son's fiancee have also been killed, he begins shooting at German soldiers. A young German captain, who understands why Rougon has gone mad, reluctantly carries out his mandate to execute civilians who take arms.

Written 1914-1915 at Harvard as part of the 'English 47 Workshop' of George Pierce Baker, where it received a student performance.

Ranald, *Eugene O'Neill Companion*, p. 642.

The Personal Equation

'A Play in Four Acts', also called *The Second Engineer*.
Written: 1915, for G. P. Baker's Harvard playwriting course.
Unperformed.
Published: in *The Unknown O'Neill*; *Complete Plays 1913-1920.*

In the New Jersey office of the IWE, Tom argues paternalistically with his girl-friend Olga, who tries to teach him a feminist viewpoint. The issue is her part in sabotaging the engines of the ship — on which Tom's father is Second Engineer. In Act II, Perkins, Tom's father, muses about the two objects he adores, his son and his ship's engines. Hearing gossip that Tom has a girl, he says he will give his house to Tom and live on the ship. In Act III, in Liverpool, sailors argue about rumours of a strike. In the engine room Perkins worries that his beloved engines may be sabotaged. The sailors try to persuade Perkins to leave so they can damage the engines. Tom is accidentally shot by his father when he leads the attack, and in Act IV lies in hospital, permanently vegetative from the wound. Olga and Perkins argue, but eventually decide to live together in the house Perkins wanted to give Tom, to care for Tom and for the baby Olga is carrying.

Have been working on my *Engineer* play, the first scenario of which you read, but the main theme has undergone such changes in my mind and wandered into such unforeseen ramifications and complications, that it has me bewildered and a bit peeved. However I hope it will all iron out in the writing

O'Neill, letter to Beatrice Ashe, 28 Mar. 1915

Before Breakfast

'A Play in One Act.'

Written: 1916, derived from Strindberg's *The Stronger*.

First performed: Playwright's Th., New York, 1 Dec. 1916 (dir. O'Neill, with help from his father; with Mary Pyne and O'Neill).

Revived: Gate Th., Dublin, 27 Feb. 1934 (dir. Hilton Edwards; with Ria Mooney); with *Hughie* and *In the Zone*, Duchess Th., London, 18 June 1963; Nameless Th., New York, Nov. 1978 (dir. Michael Alexander); American Th. Arts Conservatory, Los Angeles, Autumn 1981 (dir. Barry Bartle); Tower Th., Boston, 13 Feb. 1986 (dir. Kenneth MacDonald); No Smoking Playhouse, New York, Dec. 1986 (dir. Francisco Rivela); South Street Th., New York, 17 May 1988.

Published: in *Provincetown Plays, Third Series* (New York, 1916); *Complete Works* (1924); *Plays I*; *Complete Plays 1913-1920*.

Mrs. Rowland nags throughout the monologue at her mostly invisible husband who is shaving in the next room of their New York flat — about his laziness, their poverty, her mistake in marrying him, and his womanizing. At the end, she goes to the other room and shrieks upon finding him dead: he has evidently cut his throat with his razor.

In play after play [O'Neill] would sound the Strindbergean theme of love-hate, of the war between the sexes. . . . Perhaps the most important thing he took from Strindberg was the courage to explore in his writings the darkest corners of his own character.

Sheaffer, *O'Neill: Son and Playwright*, p. 253-4.

Now I Ask You

'A Play in Three Acts, a Prologue, and an Epilogue.'

Written: 1916.
Unperformed.
Published: in *Children of the Sea*; *Complete Plays 1913-1920*.

In a prologue-tableau Lucy holds a gun to her temple; at curtain there is 'the sound of a shot'. During the three acts, Lucy, her husband Tom, and their arty friends Leonora and Gabriel experiment with free love, but find that it bores them and that they can be as petty as the bourgeoisie they despise. At the end the gun turns out to have been unloaded and the sound of the shot came from a tire blowing out. Leonora has the last word: 'General Gabbler's [sic] pistol! Fancy that, Hedda!' The most interesting character is Lucy's mother, a Shavian heroine who manipulates the others and restores good sense. The farce works as a critique of Shaw's Ibsenism.

In the Zone

'A Play in One Act.'
Written: 1917.
First performed: Washington Square Players, Comedy Th., New York, 31 Oct. 1917 (with Frederick Roland as Smitty, Robert Strange as Davis, Jay Strong as Yank, Abram Gillette as Olson, Eugene Lincoln as Scotty, Edward Balzerit as Ivan, Arthur Hohl as Driscoll, and Rienzi de Cordova as Cocky).
First London production: on a bill with *Diff'rent*, Everyman Th., Spring 1921.
Revived: revived frequently, and toured on vaudeville circuits. See *The Long Voyage Home*.
Film and television: see *The Long Voyage Home*.
Published: in *The Moon of the Caribees*; *Plays I*; *Complete Plays 1913-1920*.

On the S. S. Glencairn, in the war zone, Smitty is suspected of being a German spy, but the 'coded messages' found by the semi-literate sailors turn out to be letters from Smitty's fiancee.

[Either just before or just after the play was written — O'Neill said after — the playwright and a friend were arrested on suspicion of being spies, their suspicious behaviour being the long walks they frequently took on the tip of Cape Cod. See Sheaffer, *O'Neill, Son and Playwright*, p. 380-4, for an account.]

The length of the dialogue was out of proportion to the substance, but the story, laid in the forecastle of a munitions ship passing through the submarine zone, contrived to create some real suspense. . . . Frederick Roland acted the suspect with commendable restraint and feeling. Arthur Hohl also scored, but nearly any one might have played the other roles as well.

New York World, 1 Nov. 1917

Ile

'A Play in One Act.'
Written: 1917.
First performed: Playwright's Th., New York, 30 Nov. 1917.
First London Performance: Everyman Th., 1921.
Revived: Greenwich Village Th., New York, 18 Apr. 1918; Santo Tomas
   Univ. Th., Manila, 1959 (with Georgina Rivera); ASTA Th.,
   Washington, D.C., Aug. 1978 (dir. Camille David); as *Huile*,
   Comedie de Caen, 1983 (mise en scène, Claude Yersin).
Opera by Beatrice Laufer, 1957.
Film and television: TV production, Peoples Republic of China, 1990.
Published: in *The Moon of the Caribees*; *Plays I*; *Complete Plays 1913-
   1920*.

[A] tale of the sea by Eugene, son of James O'Neill, the actor, entitled Ile. The O'Neill sketch is . . . set in the cabin of a whaler caught in the ice in the Behring Sea. The crew, its time worked out, is about to mutiny unless the captain gives up his unsuccessful search for 'Ile' and starts for home. He, determined to stick it out, cowers his men but weakens before the pleading of his young wife, who has accompanied him on the trip and is nigh to madness after endless months spent in gazing out over the great stretch of ice, the while she dreams of the home she has left. But just as soon as he agrees to give up the cruise, open water is reported to the northward, a school of whales is

spouting off the starboard bow, and he decides to stay. Whereupon the disappointed wife's mind gives way and he leaves her babbling incoherently as he takes to the boats. Not so good, nor so vivid, as the author's In the Zone, *being a bit obviously theatrical. But still holding claim to some part of his unusual gift for realism and red-blooded characterization.*

Burns Mantle, *New York Mail*, 19 Apr. 1918

The man O'Neill . . . knows the people of the sea and their women. He has a feeling for irony, for the sardonic humor with which the gods plot the drama of human affairs.

Louis Sherwin,
New York Globe, 19 Apr. 1918

The Long Voyage Home

'A Play in One Act.'
Written: 1917.
First performed: Provincetown Players, Playwright's Th., New York, 2 Nov. 1917 (with George Cram Cook, Ira Remsen, Hutchinson Collins, O. K. Liveright, Ida Rauh, and Alice MacDougal).
First London performance: Mercury Th., June 1947 (dir. Robert Henderson).
Revived: often with *Bound East for Cardiff, In the Zone*, and *The Moon of the Caribees*, usually as *S. S. Glencairn* or *The Long Voyage Home*; Barnstormers' Barn, Provincetown, Mass., 14 Aug. 1924; Provincetown Playhouse, New York, 3 Nov. 1924, moved to Punch and Judy Th., New York, 16 Dec. 1924, trans. to Princess Th., New York, 12 Jan. 1925 (dir. James Light; des. Cleon Throckmorton; with Sidney Machet, Lawrence Cecil, Walter Abel, Harold McGee, Walter Kingsford, E. J. Ballantyne, James Meighan, Samuel Selden, Archie Sinclair, Abraham Krainis, Mary Johns, Louise Bradley, Jeannie Begg, and Barbara Benedict); Provincetown Playhouse, New York, 1 Sept. 1929; Lafayette Th., New York, 29 Oct. 1937; New York City Center, 29 May 1948; Mermaid Th., New York, 4 Dec. 1961; Cottesloe Th., National Th., London, 20 Feb. 1979 (dir. Bill Bryden).
Film and television: United Artists, 1940 (dir. John Ford; with Thomas Mitchell as Driscoll, John Wayne as Olson, Ian Hunter as Smitty, Ward Bond as Yank, Barry Fitzgerald as Cocky, and Wilfrid Lawson as the Captain).

Published: The Moon of the Caribees; Plays I; Complete Plays 1913-1920.

Four sailors from the S. S. Glencairn *enter a London waterfront dive where they drink, flirt with the barwomen, and talk of life at sea and the next ship. Ollie wants to return to the family farm, but is shanghaied aboard a bad ship.*

[*The Moon of the Caribees*] is a remarkable work to have come from someone so young in the early years of the century. But even finer are *The Long Voyage Home* . . . and *Bound East for Cardiff*. Bill Bryden's is one of those Cottesloe productions which take risks and generally triumph in doing so. The decoy in the title play may be acted with more flamboyance than subtlety. . . . But in general this production brings home, with remarkable pathos, what the dying Yank means when he declares: 'This sailor life ain't much to cry about leavin'.'

Francis King,
Sunday Telegraph, 25 Feb. 1979

O'Neill himself was probably still on the way to engulfing pessimism, but this is recognizably the same world he was to show us in *The Iceman Cometh*. . . . We have seen meaningless celebration, lonely death, and the brutal invasion of desperate secrecy. The episodes don't all add up to good plays, but the cumulative effect is very powerful.

The plays are, for the most part, excellently presented in a style that stops craftily short of naturalism. John Salthouse as the final victim makes touching use of those uniquely Scandinavian vowels: a beamish boy snatched from the audience's arms.

Robert Cushman,
The Observer, 20 Jan. 1980

Even early on, [O'Neill's] vision is bleak and almost totally devoid of humour. The themes are loneliness, disillusionment, and the calloused hand of fate, set in a large context of the all-male kinship of men at sea. . . . [The play] exposes men's cruelty to men (and indeed to women) as a whore under male orders winkles a dumb Swede out of a two-year pay packet. . . .

Victoria Radin,
The Observer, 25 Feb. 1979

The Moon of the Caribbees

'A Play in One Act.'
Written: 1917.
First performed: Provincetown Players, Playwright's Th., New York, 20 Dec. 1918.
Revived: often. See *The Long Voyage Home.*
Film and television: see *The Long Voyage Home.*
Published: in *The Moon of the Caribbees*; *Plays I*; *Complete Plays 1913-1920.*

Virtually without story, it tells of a langorous night as the Glencairn *lies anchored off an island in the West Indies, the plaintive sound of native chants drifting in from shore. Bumboat women come aboard with rum hidden under their loads of fruit, the men pair off with them for hasty lovemaking, a donnybrook erupts among the now drunken seamen, the women are ordered ashore by the first mate, peace settles again over the ship. . . .*

Sheaffer, *O'Neill, Son and Playwright*, p. 383

[*The Moon of the Caribbees*] (my favourite [of the sea plays]) is distinctly my own. The spirit of the sea . . . is the hero.

O'Neill, letter to Barrett H. Clark, 8 May 1919

The Rope

'A Play in One Act.'
Written: 1918.
First performed: Provincetown Players, Playwright's Th., New York, 26 Apr. 1918 (dir. Nina Moise; with O. K. Liveright as Abraham, Dorothy Upjohn as Annie, and Charles Ellis as Luke).
Revived: Washington Square Players, Comedy Th., New York, 13 May 1918.
Film and television: Nederlander, 1989 (dir. Leila Swift; with Jose Ferrer as Abraham, Elizabeth Ashley as Annie, Len Cariou as Pat, and Brad Davis as Luke).
Published: in *The Moon of the Caribbees*; *Plays I*; *Complete Plays 1913-1920.*

Old Abraham Bentley hates his daughter's family, who hate him in return but tolerate him because he lets them live on the family farm. Bentley's son Luke returns from the sea, having been chased off years before by his father who wanted him to hang himself. Now appearing senile, the old man shows Luke the rope and mimes that Luke should hang himself. Luke plots with the others to torture the old man into revealing his hoard of gold. The grand-daughter, playing in the barn, finds the gold attached to the other end of the rope and throws the coins into the sea.

Beyond the Horizon

'A Play in Three Acts.'

Written: 1918. O'Neill's first major play, and the first play by an American that can justly be called a tragedy in the Greek tradition.

First performed: Morosco Th., New York, 2 Feb. 1920, trans. to Criterion Th., then to Little Th., (dir. O'Neill, replacing Richard Bennett who played Robert Mayo; with Edward Arnold as Andrew, and Helen MacKellar as Ruth).

First London performance: Everyman Th., 1921 (with Raymond Massey as Robert Mayo).

Revived: Mansfield Th., New York, 20 Nov. 1926; as *Derriere l'horizon*, Th. du Val-de-Marne, St. Maur, 1968 (mise en scène, P. Della Torre); Little Th., Queens College, Flushing, New York, 18 Mar. 1982; Source Th., Washington, D.C., 8 Nov. 1985; Palmer Aud., Connecticut College, New London, 19 Nov. 1987; Berkshire Public Th., Pittsfield, Mass., 6 Oct. 1988.

Film and television: as *Derrière l'horizon*, ORTF, 1966; PBS, 1976.

Published: Boni and Liveright, 1920; revised and cut for *Complete Works*, 1924; *Plays III; Complete Plays 1913-1920*.

The tragedy of a young, farm-born dreamer, whose romantic mind and frail body yearn for the open sea, the swarming ports of the mysterious East, the beckoning world beyond the line of hills which shut in the acres of his home. By all that is in him, he is destined for a wanderer's life, but Fate, in a wanton mood, tethers him to this little hill-cupped farm and watches coolly the misery and decay this means for all his house. You meet him first at this crossroads of his life and see him take the wrong turning.

To him, on the night before he is to set sail for a three year's cruise around the world, comes love in the form of the neighbour's daughter, whom he and all his people had thought marked rather for his brother. Blinded by the flame kindled in that moment of her confession, he lightly forgoes all thought of the world beyond the horizon, plans to settle at once on the farm with his jubilant bride, and watches serenely enough while his heart-wrenched brother sets forth on the cruise that was to have been his. . . .

Then you follow through the years the decay of that household, the tragedy of the misfit. You see the waning of love, the birth of disappointment, the corrosion of poverty and spite and disease. . . . You see the woman grow drab and dull and sullen, and you see the man, wasted by the consumption that in another life might have been avoided, crawl at last out of the hated house to die on the road he should have travelled, straining his eyes toward the hills he never crossed.

All this is told with sure dramatic instinct, clear understanding, and a certain quite unsentimental compassion. To an extent unfamiliar in our theatre, this play seems alive. This is not merely because truth works within it nor because of the realness of its people. It is rather because of the visible growth and change that take place as the play unfolds.

Alexander Woollcott, *New York Times*, 8 Feb. 1920

Shell Shock

'A Play in One Act.'
Written: 1918.
Unperformed.
Published: in *Children of the Sea*; *Complete Plays 1913-1920.*

Jack Arnold, a war hero in 'shell shock' gradually tells his story to an old friend, a medical officer. His act of heroism, Jack thinks, was really driven by a petty self-interest: he wanted a cigarette he thought he could find in a wounded man's jacket. Telling the story seems partly to cure the shell shock.

The Dreamy Kid

'A Play in One Act.'

Written: 1918.
First performed: Playwright's Th., New York, 31 Oct. 1919.
Published: in *Theatre Arts Magazine*, Jan. 1920; *Contemporary One-Act Plays of 1921*, ed. F. Shay (Cincinnati: Stewart Kidd, 1922); *Plays I*; *Complete Plays 1913-1920*.

[A] sketch which has as its central figure a young, crap-shooting, gang-leading, gun-toting darky who has just killed a white man in a scrap and who, with the police hot on his trail, has nevertheless crept to the deathbed of his grandmother, because he knows in his heart he will have no luck if he does not obey her final summons. It is interesting to see how . . . the author . . . induces your complete sympathy and pity for a conventionally abhorrent character

Alexander Woollcott, *New York Times*, 9 Nov. 1919

[Whatever the play's faults, it is notable because O'Neill took seriously his black characters, and the Provincetown Players hired a group of black players to play black roles. See Ranald, *Eugene O'Neill Companion*, p. 190, and Gelb and Gelb, p. 399-400.]

Where the Cross is Made

'A Play in One Act.'
Written: 1918.
First performed: Playwright's Th., New York, 22 Nov. 1918.
Revived: Nameless Th., New York, Fall 1978; as *L'Endroit marque d'une croix*, Comedie de Caen, 1983 (mise en scène, Claude Yersin).
Published: in *The Moon of the Caribees and Six Other Plays of the Sea* (1919); *Plays I*; *Complete Plays 1913-1920*.

Nat Bartlett wants to have his father, a sea captain, committed as insane because of an obsessive drive to go to an island where he thinks there is buried treasure: but when the father dies the obsession passes to the son.

[The play derives from an unpublished story 'The Captain's Walk', written or projected by O'Neill's second wife, Agnes Boulton. O'Neill began the four-act play *Gold* in 1919, put it aside, then revised the last act of *Gold* into the one-act *Where the Cross Is Made*.]

The Straw

'A Play in Three Acts.'

Written: 1918-19.

First performed: Greenwich Village Th., New York, 10 Nov. 1921 (with Margalo Gillmore as Eileen Carmody, Harry Harwood as Bill Carmody, and Otto Kruger as Stephen Murray).

Revived: Walker Street Repertory Th., New York, Nov. 1989 (dir. Toni Dorfman).

Published: in *The Emperor Jones, Diff'rent, The Straw* (Boni and Liveright, 1921); *Plays III*; *Complete Plays 1913-1920*.

The doctor who diagnoses Eileen Carmody's consumption forces her father to send her to a TB sanitorium, the old man protesting the cost like a James Tyrone without advantages. At the sanitorium, she meets Stephen Murray, a cynical young writer and patient with whom she falls in love. As Murray's health improves, Eileen's declines. A nurse tells Murray that Eileen will die if she learns he doesn't really love her. Murray recognizes that he does love her and proposes, even after the nurse warns that joy might be equally fatal. Murray proceeds and, as predicted, Eileen is about to die at the play's end.

The final scene . . . has a pathos and a tragic irony seldom paralleled in the theatre. After a difficult and clumsy assembling of its forces, that scene leaves the two young people together . . . jubilant in their plans for their marriage, for their flight to a little mountain lake . . . for the idyllic regime [that will cure them].

> Alexander Woollcott, *New York Times*, 11 Nov. 1921

Chris Christophersen

'A Play in Three Acts.'

Written: 1919.

First performed: entitled *Chris*, Nixon's Apollo Th., Atlantic City, New Jersey, 8 Mar. 1920, trans. to Philadelphia, 15 Mar. 1920 (dir. Frederick Stanhope, with Emmett Corrigan, Lynn Fontanne, and Arthur Ashley).

Revived: Goodman Th., Chicago, 1982.
Published: Random House, 1982; in *Complete Plays 1913-1920.*

Chris is an old [Swedish] sea-dog . . . now captain of a coal-barge. He has hated the sea for years — ever since it separated him from his wife, who died while he was away. His child, Anna, has been carefully brought up in England, and is now coming to America to meet her father. Anna arrives, and is shocked at the ugliness of the old barge which is 'home' for her father. However, she is so happy to be with her father again that Chris easily persuades her to take a trip on the barge — which she does 'for the fun of it'. Gradually she feels the call of the sea within her, and grows to love it.

They are run down in a fog by a tramp steamer, taken aboard, and carried to Buenos Aires. . . . Anna falls in love with the handsome second mate, and in spite of her father's warning decides to marry her hero. At first Chris attempts to forbid it, and even tries to kill the second mate . . . but eventually relents, and accepts the job of 'bosun' on the tramp steamer.

The material is very slim, but the play carries itself along from sheer excellence of presentation. Emmett Corrigan . . . enacts Chris with considerable skill. . . . Lynn Fontanne, as Anna, was pleasing, and her refinement did much to off-set the common coarseness of the coal-bargers.

Anonymous, The Stage, 27 Mar. 1920.

Exorcism

'A Play of Anti-Climax.'
Written: 1919.
First performed: Playwright's Th., New York, 26 Mar. 1920.
Unpublished. All copies were apparently destroyed by O'Neill.

In 1919 O'Neill wrote Exorcism, *a one-act play based on his suicide attempt. In it a bedevilled young man . . . decides to swallow poison; two drunken friends revive him and his initial despair at having been brought back to face the same dreary world changes to enlightenment and hope. . . . The play ends with his awareness that the attempted suicide has actually killed his old self and that he is a new man. . . .*

Gelb and Gelb, *O'Neill*, p. 188

Gold

'A Play in Four Acts.'
Written: 1920.
First performed: Frazee Th., New York, 1 June 1920.
Published: Boni and Liveright, 1921; revised, 1924, for *Complete Works*; *Plays II*; *Complete Plays 1913-1920*.

Captain Bartlett and five crewmen from his whaler, marooned on a coral island, find a chest of jewellery which Bartlett believes to be valuable. When a rescue ship is spotted the men quarrel, and one of them kills two others, Bartlett disclaiming responsibility. They bury the chest and Bartlett makes a map. Six months later, in Bartlett's California home, Bartlett prepares a new ship to get the treasure. His wife refuses to christen the new ship because she believes the trip is sinful and 'cursed', but Bartlett coerces her into giving her blessing to the voyage. Bartlett's daughter tricks her father into remaining ashore while her fiance sails off in the ship. Bartlett goes mad when he hears that the ship has been lost, tells his son and daughter of the murders, acknowledges his guilt, and collapses, his daughter sending her brother for a doctor at the curtain.

Anna Christie

'A Play in Four Acts.'
Written: 1919-20.
First performed: Vanderbilt Th., New York, 2 Nov. 1921 (dir. Arthur Hopkins; with Pauline Lord as Anna, George Marion as Chris, and Frank Shannon as Mat Burke).
First London production: Everyman Th., Apr.-May 1923 (with Pauline Lord).
Revived: Tribune Th., Berlin, 9 Oct. 1923; Gate Studio at the Peacock,

Dublin, 13 Jan. 1929 (dir. Hilton Edwards, who also played Chris; with Coralie Carmichael, and Fred Johnson as Mat); San Francisco, Aug. 1941 (with Ingrid Bergman); Imperial Th., New York, Apr. 1977 (dir. Jose Quintero; with Liv Ullmann); RSC, Other Place, Stratford, Oct. 1979 (dir. Jonathan Lynn; with Susan Tracy as Anna, Fulton MacKay as Chris, and Gareth Thomas as Mat); Central Academy of Dramatic Arts, Beijing, Oct. 1984 (dir. George White); Young Vic, 7 June 1990 (dir. David Thacker; with Natasha Richardson as Anna, John Woodvine as Chris, and David Herlihy as Mat).

Film and television: First National, silent, 1923 (dir. John Griffith Wray; with Blanche Sweet as Anna, George F. Marion as Chris, William Russell as Mat); MGM, 1930, (dir. Clarence Brown; with Greta Garbo as Anna, George F. Marion as Chris, Charles Bickford as Mat, and Marie Dressler as Marty); also versions of above in French and German (with additional direction by Jacque Feyder).

Published: in *The Hairy Ape, Anna Christie, The First Man* (Boni and Liveright, 1922); *Plays III*; *Complete Plays 1913-1920*.

When Chris meets his daughter in the bar he fails to see the obvious, that she is a hooker. She has been in a brothel in St. Paul, has got sick, and has come to find her father hoping to be 'staked to a rest cure'. On the coal barge Chris and Anna gradually get to know each other, Chris blaming the sea for his troubles with reverent hatred. They rescue Mat Burke from a shipwreck; he immediately falls in love with Anna, believing her when she tells him she's been a governess. Ashore, Mat charms Anna, Chris becoming increasingly jealous. There is finally a confrontation when Anna insists that both Mat and Chris acknowledge her past: she blames Chris for abandoning her and allowing her to drift into prostitution, and accuses both of being the kind of men who use women like her. Both men are shocked and reject her. Anna vows to leave, and Chris and Mat go ashore separately to get drunk. Chris returns saying he has signed up on an ocean-going ship, to return to his old life. He and Anna are reconciled. Mat returns saying he also has signed on a new ship, and he and Anna are also reconciled. It turns out Chris and Mat will be on the same ship, Anna and Mat will marry, and Anna keep a cottage for her men while they are at sea. Chris has the last words of the play: 'Fog, fog, fog, all the bloody time. You can't see vhere you vas going, no. Only dat ole davil, sea — she knows!'

[In August and September 1920, O'Neill greatly revised *Chris Chris-tophersen* (see above), keeping almost nothing but the character of Chris. In six weeks he created a completely new Anna, her new lover, a new plot, and a new title — at first he had called it *The Ole Davil*. Some reviewers found O'Neill's intentions confusing and asked questions which would preoccupy critics from then on: did O'Neill intend to be a realist? What were people to make of his characters' mysticism?]

Some people . . . think that you cannot introduce fantasy into the theatre unless you have gods and demons. After seeing Mr. Eugene O'Neill's *Anna Christie* . . . I am so drunk with fantasy extracted from hard-boiled human beings that I don't know how to become sober. . . .

[O'Neill] seems to have inside the bolus of his Irishman and his Swede a certain amount of reality. But he does not appear, on the whole, to be keenly interested in reality. He thinks it is enough to tip people's emotions up and down, especially to give them pathos and excitement. The development of his genius certainly cannot be along these theatrical lines.

Francis Hackett, The New Republic, 30 Nov. 1921

The two lovers are interlocked as the final curtain falls. . . . O'Neill seems to be suggesting to the departing playgoers that they can regard this as a happy ending if they are shortsighted enough to believe it and weak-minded enough to crave it. He, at least, has the satisfaction of intimating in his final words that, whereas everything seems cheerful enough for the moment, there is probably no end of misery for every-body hidden just ahead in the enfolding mists of the sea. It is a happy ending with the author's fingers crossed.

Alexander Woollcott, New York Times, 13 Nov. 1921

[The public seemed to think the play had a conventional happy ending, and some reviewers accused O'Neill of giving in to commercial demands. O'Neill replied in a letter to the *New York Times*.]

I wanted to have the audience leave with a deep feeling of life flowing on, of the past which is never the past — but always the birth of the future — of a problem solved for the moment but by the very nature of its solution involving new problems.

I must have failed in this attempt. . . . A kiss in the last act, a word about marriage, and the audience grow blind and deaf to what follows. No one hears old Chris when he makes his gloomy, foreboding comments on the new set of coincidences, which to him reveal the old devil sea — (fate) — up to her old tricks again. . . .

O'Neill, letter to *New York Times*, 18 Dec. 1921

The last time I saw [*Anna Christie*] was in New York when Liv Ullman's performance as the pure-souled harlot had such ringing defiance it turned the work into a feminist war-cry. But Jonathan Lynn's production . . . seems to me much nearer to O'Neill's real intentions: to write about primal human passions and the brooding influence of the sea. Occasionally his version steers towards melodrama: but that I suspect would have delighted rather than dismayed the author. . . .

Even the constant reminders of the sea (the fog, the steamers' whistles, the mournful hooting of passing ships) are not simply atmospheric but a token of the dark sexual forces at work.

Michael Billington, *The Guardian*, 12 Oct. 1979

John Woodvine's Christopherson, a powerful bear of a man who lumbers drunkenly onto the stage, speaks with a bizarre blend of accents which at first sounds unconvincing, but soon proves to be a brilliant assessment of the eclectic jumble of intonations, inflections, and expressions picked up by a Swedish sailor over years of voyaging with men of all nationalities. Woodvine combines aging physical strength with a confused emotional vulnerability, and he and Richardson present an utterly believable father-daughter relationship; both share a certain wildness and energy which neither can fully understand or control.

Helen Rose, *Plays and Players*, Sept. 1990

The Emperor Jones

'A Play in Eight Scenes.'
Written: 1920.
First performed: Playwright's Th., New York, 1 Nov. 1920, trans. to Selwyn Th., 27 Dec. 1920 (dir. George Cram Cook; with Charles S. Gilpin as Jones and Jasper Deeter as Smithers).
First London performance: Ambassadors Th., 10 Sept. 1925 (with Paul Robeson).
Revived: as *L'Empéreur Jones*, Odéon, Paris, 31 Oct. 1923 (mise en scène, G. Baty); Tribune Th., Berlin, 8 Jan. 1924; Provincetown Playhouse, New York, 5 May 1924 (with Paul Robeson); five more revivals by 1926; Abbey Th., Dublin Drama League, 16 Jan. 1927

(dir. Lennox Robinson; with Rutherford Mayne); as *L'Empéreur Jones*, Maison de la Pensée, Paris, 1949 (mise en scène, Sylvain Dhomme); Lyceum Th., Edinburgh, Aug. 1967 (dir. Gene Frankel; with James Earl Jones as Jones and Edward Zang as Smithers); Offstage Downstairs, Chalk Farm, London, Jan. 1991 (dir. Stuart Wood; with Mel Taylor).

Film and television: United Artists, 1933 (dir. Dudley Murphy; with Paul Robeson and Dudley Digges).

Opera: composed by Louis Gruenberg, Metropolitan, New York, Jan. 1933 (with Lawrence Tibbet).

Recording: Caedmon (with James Earl Jones and Stefan Gierasch), LP TRS 341 c.

Published: in *Theatre Arts Magazine*, Jan. 1921; revised, in *The Emperor Jones, Diff'rent, The Straw* (Boni and Liveright, 1921); further revised, in *Complete Works, Plays III; Complete Plays 1913-1920.*

Two years before, Jones has fled a chain gang and reached a Caribbean island by stowing away, becoming Emperor over the natives by bullying and tricking them; but in the first scene he learns they have rebelled and during the rest of the play he flees them and his own disoriented fantasies.

Jig [Cook, director of the premiere] had long dreamed of a dome, a plaster cyclorama such as advanced European theatres were using, a device that would give an illusion of spaciousness to the tiny stage at 133 MacDougal Street; but the [Provincetown] Players had never been able to afford it. . . .

With Jig and a few helpers doing all the labor, the dome cost five hundred dollars in materials alone. . . . Jasper Deeter, who was to play the Cockney trader Smithers, suggested an actor named Charles S. Gilpin . . . and after some queries in Harlem he was tracked down to Macy's where he was running an elevator. . . . He had read but a few lines at the Provincetown when all present felt he was the man for the role. . . . On several occasions in later years O'Neill told interviewers that of all the actors who had appeared in his plays, only three — Gilpin among them — had completely satisfied him.

Sheaffer, *O'Neill, Son and Artist*, p. 31-7

An odd and extraordinary play, written with imaginative genius. . . . Gilpin's is a sustained and splendid piece of acting. The moment he raises his naked body against the moonlit sky and prays is such a dark lyric of the flesh, such a cry of primitive being as I have never seen in the theatre.

Kenneth Macgowan, *New York Globe*, 4 Nov. 1920

The gigantic James Earl Jones in the Paul Robeson part sets up some exciting theatrical tension but it is bound to be a one-track affair. . . . [The] real heroes of the evening are the director, Gene Frankel, the choreographer Louis Johnson, the electronic music by Teijo Ito, and the scenery and lighting by Robin Wagner and Nicola Cernovich. For this is not best judged as straight drama. It inhabits that half-world between opera, melodrama, and ballet.

Philip Hope-Wallace, *Manchester Guardian Weekly*, 24 Aug. 1967

The play is . . . hard to bring to life in a cramped cellar on a budget of tuppence. That does not matter at the start. . . . It is enough to put actor Mel Taylor into Ruritanian red and gold, and ask him to parade beside a throne with masks carved into its woodwork.

But Taylor must spend most of the evening escaping from his unruly subjects. . . . That takes him further and further into a forest that O'Neill describes in terms of gigantic treetrunks, sinister moonbeams drifting through canopies of leaves, and 'dense low walls of underbrush'. . . . But Stuart Woods, who directs, is hard put to turn a flimsy raffia platform and some perspex hangings into either a good forest or a good forest of the mind.

Benedict Nightingale, *The Times*, 23 Jan. 1991

Diff'rent

'A Play in Two Acts.'
Written: 1920.
First performed: Playwright's Th., New York, 27 Dec. 1920, trans. to Selwyn Th., 21 Jan. 1921, to Times Square Th., 4 Feb. 1921, and to Princess Th., 7 Feb. 1921 (dir. Charles O'Brien Kennedy; with Mary Blair as Emma Crosby, James Light as Caleb Williams, and Charles Ellis as Benny Rogers).
First London Performance: on a bill with *In the Zone*, Everyman Th., Spring 1921.
Revived: Abbey Th., Dublin, 19 Mar. 1922 (dir. Lennox Robinson); Maxine Elliot's Th., New York, 25 Jan. 1938; Mermaid Th., New York, 17 Oct. 1961.

Published: in *The Emperor Jones, Diff'rent, The Straw* (Boni and
  Liveright, 1921); *Complete Works*; *Plays III*; *Complete Plays 1913-
  1920.*

*In a New England village in the 1890s, Emma Crosbie is about
to marry Caleb Williams, a whaling captain, a man she regards
as 'diff'rent' from the other men, not a hell-raiser or a
womanizer. When her brother tells her that once on a voyage
Caleb was seduced by a native girl, Emma cancels the wedding.
In Act II, thirty years later, Emma is a caricature of a flapper —
all henna, rouge, and powder — carrying on with Caleb's 23-
year-old nephew, Benny. After a confrontation Caleb hangs
himself in the barn. When Emma hears the news she goes to join
Caleb in suicide.*

There is no such performance in *Diff'rent* as Charles Gilpin gives in *The
Emperor Jones*, yet the cast is pretty evenly effective, and there is, at
least, one exceedingly good piece of acting. It is not, unfortunately, in
the part of the woman. This role [calls] for an actress who can look
sixteen [and] who can also simulate forty-six, and forty-six trying to be
young. Mary Blair plays the first act with real skill and charm. In the
second act, she does surprisingly well with what is to her almost
impossible material, but still falls far short of the necessary illusion. . . .
The honours however go to Charles Ellis as the degenerate youth . . .
[who keeps] an aspect of more or less normal and good-looking
manhood, while indicating spiritual degradation, cruelty, and lasci-
viousness by tone and glance. . .

Kenneth Macgowan, *Vogue*, 15 Mar. 1921

The First Man

'A Play in Four Acts.'
Written: 1921.
First performed: Neighborhood Playhouse, New York, 4 Mar. 1922 (dir.
  Augustin Duncan, who also played Jayson; with Margaret Mower as
  Martha).
Revived: New Vic Th., New York, Oct. 1984 (dir. Ray Huebner).
Published: in *The Hairy Ape, Anna Christie, The First Man* (Boni and
  Liveright, 1922); *Complete Works* (1924); *Plays II*; *Complete Plays.*

Originally called The Oldest Man, *the play presents the Jaysons who are about to leave on a 'five-year excavating contest' in search of the first human. Curtis doesn't know that Martha is two months pregnant. They are childless since the overwhelming loss of their daughters many years earlier. Since then Curtis has given his energy to anthropology and Martha has roamed the world with him. Curtis's Faustian search for knowledge and Martha's integrity and directness are contrasted to Curtis's petty-minded family, who suspect that his unconventional friend Bigelow is the real father of Martha's child. Curtis is upset at news of the child which he fears will interfere in the perfect union of husband and wife. When the time comes, Martha suffers childbirth alone, while Curtis hopes the baby will die, and his family gossips about the scandal they anticipate. The baby is born alive, but its size, eleven pounds, has cost Martha her life (O'Neill weighed eleven pounds at birth). Devastated by the loss of Martha, Curtis manages to accept his son with love and finds his wife living in the child.*

Its defects are positive. . . . One may call it an 'unpleasant play', but it has a vital idea, however its mechanism, characters, and language may fail. . . . It deals with the conflict of creative impulses in the modern highly-developed woman who can write books and go on exploring expeditions, but who herself feels that her supreme work is to create children. . . . Mr. Duncan [plays Curtis] with understanding but complete inability to realize the part. In the first two acts his difficulty with his lines was a stumbling block. . . . Miss Margaret Mower is a beautiful and charming creature, but never did she suggest a girl from the West who had travelled and explored, lived and loved. . . .

Maida Castellun, *New York Call*, 9 Mar. 1922

The Hairy Ape

'A Comedy of Ancient and Modern Life in Eight Scenes.'
Written: December 1921.
First Performed: Playwrights' Th., New York, 9 Mar. 1922, trans. to
   Plymouth Th., 17 Apr. (dir. James Light and O'Neill; des. Cleon
   Throckmorton and Robert Edmond Jones; with Louis Wolheim as
   Yank, Henry O'Neill as Paddy, Harold West as Long, and Mary
   Blair as Mildred).

First London Performance: Gate Th., 1928 (dir. Peter Godfrey; with George Merritt).

Revived: Tribune Th., Berlin, 31 Oct. 1924 (dir. Eugen Roberts; with Eugen Klopfer); Gate Th. at the Peacock, Dublin, 28 Oct. 1928 (dir. Hilton Edwards, who also played Yank); Uj Szinpad, Budapest, 1928; as *Le Singe velu*, Th. des Arts, Paris, 21 Sep. 1929 (mise en scène, Georges Pitoeff, who also played Yank); Comédie de l'Est, 1964 (mise en scène, H. Gignoux; music, M. Jarre); Ambassadors Th., London, 11 May 1931 (with Paul Robeson); Tao House, Danville, California, Autumn 1977 (dir. Tom G. Evans; with Jim Baird); Schaubuhne, Berlin, Nov. 1986, trans. to National Th., London, 6 May 1987 (dir. Peter Stein); Pittsburg Public Th., trans. to Berkeley Rep. Th., California, Autumn 1987 (dir. George Ferencz; music, Max Roach; with Sam Tsoutsouvas).

Film and television: United Artists, 1944 (dir. Alfred Santell; with William Bendix as Yank and Susan Hayward as Mildred).

Published: in *The Hairy Ape, Anna Christie, The First Man* (Boni and Liveright, 1922); *Complete Works* (1924); *Complete Plays.*

In the cramped stokehole the stokers speak in choric rhythm. Yank says the stokers are steam, they are steel, they belong. Long insists they are being exploited but is shouted down. Paddy ridicules the idea of 'belonging' to the soulless steel ship, and laments the lost days of sail. On the promenade deck Mildred and her aunt bicker about Mildred dabbling in social work. An officer takes Mildred on a tour of the stokehole. In the stokehole Yank whips his team into frenzied stoking, but is suddenly aware that the other stokers are looking at something behind him. He turns, snarling, to see Mildred in her white dress. Terrified, she faints calling Yank 'a filthy beast.' He in turn is stunned to see himself as she sees him, as a crazed animal.

As Yank sits in the pose of Rodin's 'Thinker', Long and Paddy analyze Mildred's effect on Yank, Yank becoming enraged. On Fifth Avenue, where manikin men and women pass all around the raging Yank and Long, Yank tries to punch a man. The man is unhurt but the police are called and Long flees as Yank becomes increasingly violent. In prison Yank, again in the pose of the thinker, says that if steel doesn't belong, he will become the fire that melts steel. He tries to join an IWW local, but is suspected of being an 'agent provacateur' and thrown out. At last he goes to the gorilla cage in the zoo. He envies the ape as a creature who once belonged, lets it out of the cage, and tries to shakes its hand.

The ape crushes Yank and wanders off, leaving the reader with a final stage direction: 'And perhaps the Hairy Ape at last belongs'.

No actor we know could roar more effectively, swear with more freedom and give less offence, or suggest the pathetic groping of a primitive human better than [Wolheim as Yank].

> Burns Mantle,
> *New York Mail*, 10 Mar. 1922

I didn't want to sell [movie rights for *The Hairy Ape*] because I knew no one in Hollywood had the guts to film my play, do it as a symbolic expressionism as it should be done, and not censor it into imbecility, or make it a common realistic stoker story. I remember that its first stage production was one of my most satisfying times in the theatre. I remember Wolheim was practically perfect as 'Yank', and was also a pal of mine, I don't want to have that memory spoiled [by seeing the movie].

> O'Neill, letter to Teresa Helburn,
> 16 May 1944

The first Yank in 1922 was a former American football star with a bashed boxer's nose, who had fought with Pancho Villa in Mexico, taught maths at Cornell, and once brawled to such effect that he had to be restrained by four policemen outside the Astor Hotel. Times change. Mr. [Roland] Schafer is not like that at all, a powerful, muscular, humorous and wholly intelligent member of the Schaubuhne ensemble who avoids all ethnic contentiousness and ensures that Stein's production is entirely faithful to both spirit and letter of O'Neill's favourite play. I cannot imagine it better done. . .

> Michael Ratcliffe,
> *The Observer*, 7 Dec. 1986

The Fountain

'A Play in Eleven Scenes.'
Written: 1921-22.
First Performed: Greenwich Village Th., New York, 10 Dec. 1925 (dir. and des., Robert Edmond Jones; with Walter Huston as Juan Ponce de Leon, Egon Brecher as Luis, and Rosalind Fuller as Beatriz).

Revived: Abbey Th., Dublin, 6 May 1928 (dir. Dennis Johnston).
Published: in *The Great God Brown, The Fountain, The Moon of the Caribbees, and Other Plays* (New York: Boni and Liveright, 1926); in *Plays I*; in *Complete Plays 1920-1931*.

Juan, hearing of the fountain of youth, leaves his mistress Maria in Granada to join Columbus. He governs Porto Rico [sic] for twenty years, feuding with Bishop Menendez over policy toward the Indians. An Indian, Nano, tells him a story of a fountain which reminds him of the Moorish tale that set him travelling. Beatriz, daughter of Maria and Juan's ward, comes from Spain; between her and the idea of the fountain, Juan's will is restored. He leads a voyage to seek Cathay and they find land which Juan calls Florida. Wounded after several skirmishes with Indians, Juan sees a vision of Beatriz and the fountain to which people of all religions come. In a Cuban monastery, Beatriz brings her fiance, Juan's nephew, whom the dying Juan recognizes as his own youthful self: such is the true nature of the fountain of youth.

The role of Ponce de Leon fell to Mr. Walter Huston, and over his performance there will be many diverse opinions. The part fitted obviously the obvious romantic actor, and, to tell the truth, its theatrical fortunes might have gained in other hands than Mr. Huston's. But to me he seemed a piece of good casting, taken all in all. . . .

If Mr. Huston lacked often distinct style and rhythm, he had something for such a part much more significant. I mean a certain authority of character. He knew intelligently what the rock-bottom of the role was about. He had no hint of the actor ass, almost inevitable in such a part. He has a fine natural voice and a direct virility of attack. His method is sometimes thin and dry, but it is pure. Even when he is bad he could always be bad in so much worse a way. Seeing his Ponce de Leon we may say that as an artist he has the youth and truthful vigour of this New World; what he needs now also is more of the Old World's rich investiture.

Stark Young, *The New Republic*, 30 Dec. 1925

Welded

'A Play in Three Acts.'

Written: 1922-23.

First Performed: 39th Street Th., New York, 17 Mar. 1924 (dir. Stark Young; des. Robert Edmond Jones; with Doris Keane as Eleanor Cape and Jacob Ben-Ami as Michael).

Revived: Horace Mann Th., Columbia University, New York, 10 June 1981 (dir. Jose Quintero; with Philip Anglim as Michael and Ellen Tobie as Eleanor).

Published: in *All God's Chillun Got Wings and Welded* (New York: Boni and Liveright, 1924); revised, in *Complete Works* (1924); *Plays II*; *Complete Plays 1920 -1931*.

One of O'Neill's interesting failures. As the Capes talk of the new play he is writing for her to perform, they become lost in passion until a knock at the door disturbs them. John, who directs Eleanor in Michael's plays, has come to ask questions about the new play. When he leaves, Michael explodes at Eleanor for answering the door. Passion for his wife turns to suspicion of John, and then to a conviction that the ideal of intimacy of the marriage has been betrayed. Each rushes out intent on adultery. Eleanor goes to John and tries to seduce him but cannot go through with it; Michael does the same with an unnamed 'Woman'. In Act III the Capes endure the return swing of their pendulum, embracing in love at the final curtain.

The problem with Eleanor is to make the emotions ring true. She can't be played as sensible or philosophical, even if her part is full of philosophical talk, because the talk is stilted and doesn't make sense when read as logic. But if she is played as being in the grip of an overwhelming passion that she can't understand, you can capture that half-raving quality of her speeches.

You have to play her as so self-involved that the audience might laugh at her, but she should never be aware of what's funny. The character is quite Chekhovian in that way. In the first scene of the second act, she stomps all over John without meaning to; she just isn't paying any attention to him. If, in any way, she could seem to know what she is doing to him, she would be horrible. There is no emotional justification in the play for her to be humiliating John, consciously; that knowingness would add another dimension to the play which doesn't exist, so you have to be careful. . . .

Stephanie Greene, 'An Actress Talks about *Welded*', *Eugene O'Neill Newsletter*, Summer-Fall 1981

The Ancient Mariner

Written: 1923, as adaptation from Coleridge.

First performed: Provincetown Playhouse, New York, 6 Apr. 1924 (dir. and des. Robert Edmond Jones and James Light; with E. J. Ballantine as the Mariner).

Published: in *Yale University Library Gazette*, XXXV (1960), p. 61-86.

O'Neill presents the Mariner, wedding guests, and sailors in masks or stylized makeup and costumes, and the albatross as, first, the 'Dove of the Holy Ghost'; later, 'a figure all in white planes like a snow crystal'; last, a white cross hung on the Mariner.

Under the delusion that he made a dramatization of Coleridge's [poem], what Eugene O'Neill has actually made was a moving picture. What drama lies in the poem, he extracted, and in its place put a series of cut-backs and fade-outs . . . to convert the whole thing into a film of the popular order.

George Jean Nathan, The American Mercury, June 1924

The Ancient Mariner was part of a deliberate experiment in the development of a theatrical experience resulting from the joint skills of designer, director, and playwright to create spectacle and a total involvement of the senses of the audience without dependence on the actor or on the text.

Ranald, Handbook, p. 22-3

All God's Chillun Got Wings

Written: 1923.

First performed: Provincetown Playhouse, New York, 15 May 1924, trans. to Greenwich Village Th., 18 Aug. 1924 (dir. James Light; with Paul Robeson as Jim and Mary Blair as Ella),

First London performance: Gate Th., 13 Mar. 1926 (dir. Peter Godfrey).

Revived: Kamerny Th. of Moscow, Th. Pigalle, Paris, May 1930; Circle in the Square, New York, Mar. 1975.

Opera: composed by John Frans Ruivenkamp copyrighted 1982.

Published: in *All God's Chillun Got Wings and Welded* (Boni and Liveright, 1924); *Complete Works* (1924); *Plays*; *Complete Plays 1920-1931*.

In the first scene, black and white children play in a New York slum, ethnic traits emphasized by songs and racial slurs; the black Jim Harris and the white Ella Downey are teased for their friendship. Nine years later Ella, now Mickey's girl, hates 'coloured people'; studious and intelligent, Jim seems 'queerly baffled', as he is throughout his life, by the complex warfare between blacks and kindly whites. Five years later, Ella has had Mickey's child, which has died, and she has apparently become a prostitute, and Mickey is washed up as a fighter. She meets Jim when he has just failed the law exam again; he pities her sadness and illness, offers to marry her, and she accepts. Jim collapses in gratitude when she agrees, and says he will be 'your black slave that adores you as sacred'. Act I concludes with their marriage a few weeks later. Two years later, visiting with her husband's mother and sister, Ella is crumbling, flinching with dread from an African mask, and insisting she will not let Jim take and fail the law exams again. Six months later Ella is insane and tries to kill Jim, who refuses his sister's advice to have Ella committed. In the last scene, Jim thanks God for 'the child You sent me for the woman You take away' because the fire of his ordeal will 'purify' him. At the end Ella, like the child in the first scene, begs Jim to come play make-believe with her, and he says they will play until they die.

[O'Neill] understands one aspect of the 'negro problem', but he succeeds in giving this problem universality, in implying a wider application, . . . in implying . . . the universal problem of differences which create a mixture of admiration, love, and contempt, with consequent tension. At the same time, he has never deviated from exact portrayal of a possible negro, and the close is magnificent.

T. S. Eliot, on the published text, *The Criterion*, Apr. 1926

[After reports that a white woman would kiss a black actor's hand on the New York stage, O'Neill and his colleagues received death threats from the Ku Klux Klan and others while the play was in rehearsal.]

All God's Chillun Got Wings . . . finally made its way to the stage of the Provincetown Playhouse last night, where instead of causing a riot, it was greeted with cheers and loud whistlings. Possibly if it had not been made so notorious its welcome would have been calmer. It is not a play to arouse great enthusiasm.

Certainly there had been no enthusiasm for it at the Mayor's office during the day, for the directors of the theatre had applied for a permit to use a group of children in the first scene and the permit had been refused, no explanation being offered. . . . James Light, who staged the play, merely read the first scene [to the audience] and the drama proceeded as if nothing had happened.

Arthur Pollock, Brooklyn Daily News, 16 May 1924

Mr. Eugene O'Neill has at last hit upon tragedy. He has the theme, the intensity, the terror and exaltation. All this will be missed by those who see the play through a curtain of words. Such words as miscegenation, for instance. It will be missed by those who indulge in sociological reflections. Mr. O'Neill has fortunately gone much deeper. . . .

The production of the Provincetown Players is notably fine. Mr. Paul Robeson is a superb actor, extraordinarily sincere and eloquent. Miss Mary Blair was a little halting in the earlier scenes; later she rose to the occasion and was literally thrilling at moments. . . . I have seen far more beauty and intelligence and mobility than there are in this production and this play. I have seen nothing that so deeply gave me an emotion comparable to what the Greeks must have felt at the dark and dreadful actions set forth by the older Attic dramatists.

Lewis Lewisohn, The Nation, 4 Jun. 1924

Desire under the Elms

'A Play in Three Parts.'
Written: 1924.
First performed: Greenwich Village Th., New York, 11 Nov. 1924 (dir. Robert Edmond Jones; with Walter Huston as Ephraim Cabot, Charles Ellis as Eben, and Mary Morris as Abbie).
First London performance: Gate Th., 24 Feb. 1931 (with George Merritt as Ephraim, Flora Robson as Abbie, and Eric Portman as Eben): this was given as a 'private' performance, to avoid the 1925 ban of the Lord Chamberlain's Office; first public performance in 1940.
Revived: Kamerny Th. of Moscow, Th. Pigalle, Paris, May 1930; Gate Th., Dublin, 15 Feb. 1944 (dir. Hilton Edwards); Nemzeti Színhás,

Budapest, 1946; ANTA Playhouse, New York, 16 Jan. 1952; as
Désir sous les ormes, Comédie des Champs Elysée, Paris, 1953
(adapt. Jean Anouilh; mise en scène, C. Sainvall); Th. Polski,
Warsaw, 10 Feb. 1961; Circle in the Square Th., New York, 8 Jan.
1963; Greenwich Th., London, 6 May 1987 (dir. Patrick Mason; with
Tom Hickey as Ephraim, Colin Firth as Eben, and Carmen de Sautoy
as Abbie); Denver Center Th., with the Japan Foundation, Oct. 1989,
trans. to Hakuhinkan Th., Ginza, Japan, Nov. 1989, followed by
tours of Osaka, Nagoya, and Kyoto (dir. Donovan Marley; with Jim
Baker as Ephraim, Jacqueline Antaramian, and Scott Quintard as
Eben).

Film: Paramount, 1958 (dir. Delbert Mann; with Burl Ives as Ephraim,
Sophia Loren as Anna [sic], and Anthony Perkins as Eben).

Published: in *Collected Works* (1924); *Desire under the Elms* (Boni and
Liveright, 1925); *Plays I*; *Complete Plays 1920-1931*.

---

*It is 1850 on a New England farm, and old Ephraim Cabot, as
stony as his hostile acres, is bringing 'hum' a bride, his third.
Two sons by his 'fust' wife, foreseeing their disinheritance, start
for the gold fields of California, leaving Eben, their handsome
stepbrother, to face his new 'ma'. She is an odd New Englander,
a combination of hot blood and cold heart. Casting her
inscrutable eyes on Eben's pleasing person, she devises a means
to be happy though married.*

Aided by her stepson's hatred for his grim father, she seduces the
boy, and as a consequence of that misbehaviour has a child by him.
Later in the play, when life as Mr. O'Neill sees it comes to grips with
life, she murders the babe, thinking to please the irresolute Eben. That
action at first horrifies him, and he gives her up to the constables. All the
time this is going on, Mr. O'Neill's black and fascinating wings hover
above the drama [i.e., the elm trees that frame the set of the house]. But
at the end [Eben] returns to the kisses of her thin, red lips and goes, so
far as I know, to the gallows with her. . . .

So alarming an interpretation of Nature is [the play] that even the
most hardened of Mr. O'Neill's disciples last night shuddered at its
honest terror and were subdued

Percy Hammond, *New York Herald Tribune*, 12 Nov. 1924

In Mr. Mason's production you get plenty of desire but no elms. He
ignores O'Neill's very precise stage directions with their description of
two overshadowing trees with 'a sinister maternity in their aspect'.

Instead he and Mr. Vanek frame the action inside an enormous, V-shaped barn with Mick Hughes's footlights throwing looming shadows on the back wall. It is a daring device, but it works, partly because it removes the taint of *Cold Comfort Farm* rustic melodrama and partly because it reminds us how much the early O'Neill deals in dominant themes and images. In *The Hairy Ape* it is steel and solitude; in *Desire under the Elms* it is stone and solitude.

The latter is a less good play because you sense O'Neill straining for tragic effect (the murder of the child is abrupt and implausible). But, in Mr. Mason's production, the farm takes on symbolic overtones of America where acquisitive ownership battles against shared love.

And there is an extraordinary performance from Tom Hickey . . . as Ephraim: a stiff-gaited old pentecostal puritan capable of sudden bursts of manic vitality. Carmen Du Sautoy catches both Abbie's land-hunger and sexy languor, and Colin Firth's Eben is suitably guilt-ridden and Oedipal. But what is astonishing, seeing Mason and Stein's productions [of *The Hairy Ape*] back to back is the raw theatrical power of 'twenties O'Neill and his ability to capture poetically the doomed loneliness of American life whether on a New England farm or in the concrete environs of New York.

Michael Billington, *The Guardian*, 13 May 1987

In the Greenwich Theatre production, a barn-like set equipped with the meagre minimum of tattered furnishings and battered utensils, displays the grinding improverishment of New England subsistence farming. On the floor, pebbles are strewn — significantly, since stone infuses this play as much as iron does *The Hairy Ape*. Characters hurl handfuls of shale in frustration; a rock is raised in menace; talk of stone walls, stony soil, and flinty behaviour tumbles out.

Like *The Hairy Ape*, this play grinds the animal against the mineral. Human gorillas trapped in iron are replaced — as Patrick Mason's production points up — by bovine stock painfully penned in by their farm's walls. Colin Firth, all sudden movements and aggressively blurted speech, shows one of them, Eben, as at the end of his tether. Like Yank, he is driven by a rage for revenge that is also self-assertion. But where the earlier play dealt with obsession, this is about possession. Eben — Firth fiercely demonstrates — wants to possess the family farm. He loses it because he possesses his father's new wife.

Carmen Du Sautoy reveals the different kinds of possessiveness clutching her. At first, she strays proprietorially round the home she's bought by marriage, almost sensually rubbing herself up against the woodwork and fondling the furniture. As her patriarchal husband, Tom Hickey — looking like a leprechaun and sounding like an imitation of

American Bible Belt rant overheard in a Dublin pub very near closing time — has none of the granite tyranny the part requires. Elsewhere, though, sparks are constantly struck from the drama's stony scenes.

Peter Kemp, *The Independent*, 13 May 1987

Marco Millions

Written: 1923-24, abridged version 1925.
First performed: Guild Th., New York, 9 Jan. 1928 (dir. Rouben Mamoulian; with Alfred Lunt as Marco Polo).
First London performance: Westminster Th., 1938 (dir. Michael MacOwan).
Revived: Liberty Th., New York, 3 Mar. 1930; ANTA Washington Square Th., New York, 20 Feb. 1964; Nemzeti Színhás, Pecs, Hungary, 1973; Th. Montparnasse, Paris, 1973 (mise en scène, M. C. Valene); Shanghai People's Arts Th., China, 1988.
Published: Marco Millions (Boni and Liveright, 1927); *Plays II*; *Complete Plays 1920-1931*.

Marco Millions, *first called 'Marco's Millions', was originally written in eight acts (14 scenes) and an epilogue, and would have run about six hours. When it was rejected by the producer David Belasco, O'Neill condensed the play to eleven scenes, divided into four acts and the epilogue. Like* The Fountain, *it recalls Ibsen's* Peer Gynt *in its characters' worldwide wandering and its mingling of eastern and western metaphysics.*

The most elaborate of the new American plays, as well as by far the most glamorous, is . . . *Marco Millions*, which has finally come to a generous and abundant production at the hands of the Theatre Guild. As everyone knows by now, *Marco* is the story of Babbitt retold in ancient dress, wherein the smoking-car wit and the Rotarian complacency of the Polos . . . are set against the splendour and the mystic wisdom of the court of Kublai, the Great Kaan. . . . O'Neill has not admitted satire as his final goal. Instead he has written with a haunting and savage beauty that lifts the play far above the mockery which is ordinarily aimed at Kiwanians. . . . [The play suffers from] that incapacity of [O'Neill] to give his plays final finish . . . which permits him to let his last act, both in the acting and printed versions, slough off into the grandiose phrases of a deeply felt but weakly thought mysticism. . . . Of the actors it is

Alfred Lunt who blurs the script most, by making fatigue a characteristic of his Marco, who in the text is still unformed and capable of both imagination and emotion. . . . Of the many acute characterizations, Dudley Digges's shrivelled Cathayan sage, Chu-Yin, stands out in the highest relief, cold with the imperturbability of the East and wise with the wisdom of the ages.

John Mason Brown, *Theatre Arts*, Mar. 1928

The Great God Brown

Written: 1925.
First performed: Greenwich Village Th., New York, 23 Jan. 1926,
    moved to Garrick Th., New York, 1 Mar. 1926; trans. to Klaw Th.,
    10 May 1926 (dir. Robert Edmond Jones; with William Harrigan as
    Brown, Robert Keith as Dion, Leona Hogarth as Margaret, and Anne
    Shoemaker as Cybel).
First London performance: Gate Th., 1927 (dir. Peter Godfrey; with
    John Gielgud as Dion, Hugh Williams as Brown, Moyna MacGill as
    Margaret, and Mary Clare as Cybel).
Revived: Coronet Th., New York, 6 Oct. 1959; New Phoenix Co., New
    York, 1972; Germinal Th., Denver, Autumn 1977 (dir. E. Baierlein).
*Published: The Great God Brown, The Fountain, The Moon of the
    Caribees and Other Plays* (Boni and Liveright, 1926); *Plays III*;
    Complete Plays 1920-1931.

The schoolboy Billy Brown loves Margaret, who loves and marries Dion Anthony — but she loves his mask, and avoids knowing the pain and exposed nerves beneath. Dion has impulses to create beautiful buildings, but no sense of form: he depends on the plodding Brown to organize his impulses.

It is not [O'Neill's] fashion to bargain with his dreams in the interests of black and white playwriting. And now that he has striven to increase the stature of drama so that it may catch the full richness of his emotion, he puts a responsibility upon his audience too great and far too flattering. For two acts *The Great God Brown* makes its esoteric points with translucent clarity, and meanwhile pours a flood of powerful feeling across the footlights. When the masks for each individual increase from one to two in the remaining acts, and quick shifts are made from one to the other or from mask to real flesh, and the play cuts loose entirely from reality, the result is quite bewildering. . . . Indeed, if every line in the play did not ring with passion and sincerity, the complexity of this mode of expression might engender impatience in the mind of the play-goer. . . . [But] in the presence of so much genuine honesty of purpose, one willingly concedes Mr. O'Neill the benefit of the doubt and merely observes that *The Great God Brown* is in large part inarticulate. . . .

The personal radiance of Miss Hogarth in the part of Margaret contrasts wonderfully with the phlegmatic countenance of her mask. Similarly, in the part of Dion Mr. Keith imbues his acting of the real man with an interior distress that sets off the surface mockery of his mask. As Cybel, the prostitute and the symbol of Mother Earth, Miss Shoemaker plays with an extraordinary pity, understanding, and gentleness.

Brooks Atkinson, *New York Times*, 25 Jan. 1926

If Mr. O'Neill writes for anything beyond the satisfaction of his own urge, it is for posterity, not for popularity. Here he experiments bravely and strangely. . . . It is the fate of O'Neill, in so many of his plays, to imprison himself in some technical scheme. . . . The wild soulful theme of *The Great God Brown* is ball-and-chained to this embarrassing trickery of masks. The actors are adept at using them. Once you are used to them, and to the muffled tones behind them, you accept them as implicitly as you can. But they are never wholly free from difficulty, always a thorn in your imagination.

Gilbert W. Gabriel, *New York Sun*, 25 Jan. 1926

They are not the stylized masks of custom, but careful duplicates of the faces of those who wear them, as individual as their own features but stiff with the rigidity of deathly life. These grim mummies are put on and off throughout the play, changing its aspect when they are changed. A whole scene is transformed as a character slips out, his face naked and unashamed, to startle those about him with the sudden terror of reality. Yet the mechanics of all this are not grotesque. It is a convention easy enough to accept in principle, and difficult only when the playwright carries it to an extreme of baffling complications by allowing one character to steal the mask of another he has killed.

John Anderson, *New York Post*, 25 Jan. 1926

[In the 'stunning' Germinal Th. production] clear plastic masks are used and are unusually effective. Without obscuring the actors' faces, the masks completely alter each individual's features enough to suggest total transformation. . . .

Barbara Mackay, *New York Theatre Review*, Dec. 1977

Lazarus Laughed

'A Play for an Imaginative Theatre.'
Written: 1925-26.
First performed: Pasadena Playhouse, California, 9 Apr. 1928
(dir. Gilmor Brown, who also played Tiberius; with Irving Pichel as Lazarus, Dore Wilson as Pompeia, Lenore Shanewise as Miriam, Victor Jory as Caligula, and Maurice Wells as Marcellus and the Father of Lazarus).
Revived: Collins Auditorium, Fordham University, New York, 8 Apr. 1948; University of California, Berkeley, 1950.
Published: Act I in *The American Caravan: a Yearbook of American Literature*, ed. Van Wyck Brooks, L. Mumford, et al. (New York: Macaulay, 1927); *Lazarus Laughed* (Boni and Liveright, 1927); *Plays I*; *Complete Plays 1920-1931*.

In form Lazarus Laughed *is a Greek tragedy, while the import is not unlike the mystery plays which used to be done during the Middle Ages. The story undertakes to reveal what O'Neill believes followed the raising of Lazarus from the dead by Jesus. Being the first man to return from the realm whose boundary is never supposed to be recrossed, the multitude hangs upon Lazarus's words. He tells them that there is no death — only God's eternal laughter. That is the burden of the whole play. The succeeding scenes represent a series of tests by the Jews, Romans, and Greeks to try Lazarus' faith. In turn the various members of his family are taken from him, but he continues ever to laugh, even to the end when Emperor Tiberius has him burned at the stake. . . .*

A unit setting, designed by James Hyde, was manipulated for all eight scenes. Its proportions were such as to dominate the play at all times. Although the script does not call for a musical score, one was provided by Arthur Alexander, which added to the emotional effect. . . . Irving Pichel . . . [played Lazarus] in a stereotyped Christ-like manner, which hardly seems to be the Dionysian sort of man the author had in mind. . . . From a production standpoint *Lazarus Laughed* must be hailed as an achievement more than compensating what it lacked in the way of satisfactory acting. Several hundred supernumeraries contributed to the mise en scène, which was effectively handled, colourfully costumed, and for the most part notably lighted.

H. O. Stechan, *Billboard*, 21 Apr. 1928

You are right to ask who can play 'Laz'. No one that I know of who has ever played in the States except Chaliapin. He would be magnificent, I think, but he is quite money-mad and impossible to interest (except commercially), so they say. And he doesn't know English. But I wouldn't care about that. He could speak the lines in Russian. The average audience would probably get just as much out of them that way! All in all I'm not expecting much from an American production of this play but I do think they will do well by it in Russia — that there are actors there who have the talent, and have had the training, to play Lazarus. All the Russians who have read it or had it read to them — Danchenko, for example — have been particularly keen about it. Their strong religious feeling about life, I suppose.

O'Neill, letter to Benjamin de Casseres, 22 June 1927

My best bet for [Spencer] Tracy would be *Lazarus Laughed*. Now give heed to this and reread it carefully in the light of what that play has to say today. 'Die exultantly that life may live,' etc. 'There is no death' (spiritually) etc. Also think of the light thrown on different facets of the psychology of dictators in Tiberius and Caligula. Hitler doing his little dance of triumph after the fall of France is very like my Caligula.

As far as the unreal-realistic paraphernalia of the masked mobs, chorus, etc., is concerned, forget that. We'll throw all that out. Use only a few people, the rest all offstage sound — unseen choir effect. Boris Godunov as a hint of the method. Oh yes, I mean with music. No one but Chaliapin [who had died in 1938] could ever do Lazarus's laughter, but it could be done by exultant music so that you get the feeling the music is his laugh.

O'Neill, letter to Lawrence Langner, 31 Dec. 1943

Strange Interlude

Written: 1926-27.
First performed: John Golden Th. New York, 30 Jan. 1928, (The Theatre Guild, dir. Philip Moeller, des. Jo Mielziner, with Tom

Powers as Marsden, Lynn Fontanne as Nina, Earle Larimore as Sam, and Glenn Anders as Darrell), 426 performances.

First London performance: Lyric Th., 1931.

Revived: Vígsínhás, Budapest, 1929; Actors' Studio, Hudson Th., New York, 11 May 1963 (dir. Jose Quintero; with Geraldine Page, Ben Gazzarra, and Pat Hingle); Duke of York's Th., London, 6 Apr. 1984 (dir. Keith Hack; des. Voytek; with Edward Petherbridge as Marsden, Glenda Jackson as Nina, Brian Cox as Darrell, and James Hazeldine as Sam); National Th., Brussels, May 1988.

Film and television: MGM, 1932 (dir. Robert Z. Leonard; with Ralph Morgan as Marsden, Norma Shearer as Nina, Clark Gable as Darrell, and Alexander Kirkland as Sam); HTV, July 1988 (dir. Herbert Wise; with Edward Petherbridge as Marsden, Glenda Jackson as Nina, Jose Ferrer as Prof. Leeds, David Dukes as Darrell, and Ken Howard as Sam).

Recording: Columbia Records (dir. Jose Quintero; with Geraldine Page as Nina, William Prince as Marsden, Ben Gazzara as Darrell, Pat Hingle as Sam, Richard Thomas as Gordon, and Jane Fonda as Madeline), LP 688.

Published: Strange Interlude (Boni and Liveright, 1928); in *Plays I*; *Complete Plays 1920-1931*.

O'Neill's nine-act marathon occurred in the John Golden Theatre yesterday, when the Theatre Guild presented *Strange Interlude* at an afternoon and night session which took a total of five hours to pass a given point. As matters of possibly historical importance it may be reported that the survivors, at the end, seemed in good health, though withered, and that Mr. Otto Kahn and Professor Max Reinhardt achieved the ultimate in sartorial nicety by changing to dress clothes during the dinner hour, while others, less favoured, merely changed the subject. . . .

Admit that it is an ordeal by watered dialogue; admit that its sprawling size does, at times, convict O'Neill of reckless waste and artistic laziness — call it even vain of its own huge bulk, and yet, and yet . . . it does manage to be profoundly engrossing, with the hypnotic fascination of seeing four people live out their tangled and twisted lives against a background of their own motives, and to the spoken chorus of their own thoughts. . . . It is a cumbersome, and sometimes a ridiculously awkward procedure, managed mechanically by a change in voice, and the sudden halt of all motion on the stage, so that the scenes take on, intermittently, the jerky attitude of a self-starting wax works. . . .

With this elaborate structure O'Neill tells the story of a woman and three men who are, in her eyes, her father, her husband, and her lover. She marries one to forget a dead aviator she once loved, and has a son by another when she finds that her husband's family is tainted with insanity. . . .

[Miss Fontanne, playing in the principle part, acts with vitality and sustained brilliance; Mr. Anders portrays Darrell with repressed intensity and adroitness of understanding.] Mr. Mielziner has provided lovely settings, Mr. Moeller has given it sensitive and often splendidly effective direction, and the audience gave it perhaps the most patient and consecutive ear ever assembled in this town, even if one croupy old lady near your reviewer did seem to think that she was a member of the cast and spoke her thoughts right out, as if they might have been no more than subtitles.

John Anderson,
New York Evening Journal, 31 Jan. 1928

From the standpoint of technique *Strange Interlude* is, of course, of the very highest interest. It succeeds by means both of its unusual length and its novel uses of spoken thought in presenting upon the stage a kind of story hitherto capable of being treated in the novel alone, and it may possibly establish a new kind of dramatic writing if others can be found to master its form as O'Neill has mastered it. Yet the importance of the play considered as an isolated work does, nevertheless, consist essentially in the fact that it approaches, as perhaps no other modern play approaches, true tragedy without imitating Greek or Elizabethan forms, and without adopting any archaic point of view. It arrests and startles its auditors because it moves them in a new way of making possible for moderns something which must be analogous to the experience undergone when the great tragedies of the past were not only great as literature but intimately related to the spirit of the age which produced them, because, in short, it treats modern life in a fashion convincingly heroic. There are many dramas written during the twentieth century of which it may be truthfully said that they are interesting, subtle, or true; of what other contemporary play can it be said that it is also and in all senses of the word 'great'?

Joseph Wood Krutch,
New York Herald Tribune, 11 Mar. 1928

When the [premiere] performance broke at seven-thirty for its single intermission, [Kenneth] Macgowan and his wife hurried to the Wentworth [Hotel], where they dined with O'Neill and gave him a heartening account of their impressions and the evident audience response. Though he appeared less tense after hearing them out, the only time he smiled was when Kenneth mentioned that a drugstore near the theatre was advertising 'Strange Interlude sandwiches'. 'I know what that is', the playwright cracked. 'It's a four-decker with nothing but ham.'

Louis Sheaffer, *O'Neill, Son and Artist*, p. 287

[The characters speak their thoughts aloud not] to the audience, that was the novelty, for we merely overhear them. We catch the characters at it, and since the lifting of masks is not only a matter for shock but for laughter too, the most important thing about this revival is that it crackles with comedy of the most bracing sardonic kind throughout. These Yankees are sharp. Petherbridge is very funny indeed as the Jamesian male auntie, composer of decorous novels, all agonising and indestructibility, while one of the most extraordinary themes occurs at the end of the third act. Nina and Ned seek to detach themselves from reality — and therefore from conventional blame — as they plan the fathering of Sam's child, tenderly shifting grammatical cases and tenses as they approach their actual selves: this is performed with tight-rope virtuosity, just this side of the absurd, by Miss Jackson and Mr Cox.

The show looks stunning. Mr. Hack's production unfolds on a series of beautiful days in spring, summer, and fall inside a dappled clapboard box which doubles as the blue skies and scudding clouds of New England's Atlantic coast (Voytek with Michael Levine), a perfect translucent space within which the bones of O'Neill's dramatic radiography can glow.

Michael Ratcliffe,
The Observer, 8 Apr. 1984

Eugene O'Neill never intended that *Strange Interlude* should be regarded as soap opera. If Herbert Wise and the mini-series had not crossed his path, the thought that it might be would never have occurred to us. But led into television's big parade, presented as a three-part serial, the similarities of material and of construction are inescapable. We are obliged to assess O'Neill from an entirely new standpoint: why is this better soap than *Dynasty* or *The Colbys*? . . .

How is this farrago superior to modern soap? What rescues O'Neill from this humiliating propinquity? . . . The superiority is in the language. O'Neill does not use language as a kind of policeman pointing the way to which characters have come and gone; or as an instrument for reporting what they said or did . . . . In O'Neill's hands, language is like a stick reflectively stirring the mud of imagination, working much as a ghost story works, by suggesting there is more out there in the darkness of the human mind than we normally admit, particularly when it

concerns doomed searches for happiness. Even where the psychological conclusion is no longer plausible, the poetic drama works on the mind. . . .
Peter Lennon, *The Listener*, 21 July 1988

In spite of its length and unrelenting morbidity, it provides a fascinating look into the mind of one of America's most ambitious playwrights. But first the viewer must adjust to the static nature of the work and the endless verbal interplay between what the characters are thinking (and articulating to the audience) and what they are actually saying to each other. . . .

For most of [the] characters, 'the present is an interlude in which we call upon the past and future to bear witness that we are living.' . . . Early in the play [Nina] claims that 'the mistake was made when God was created in the image of man. . . . Men should have been more gentlemanly and remembered their mothers', before assigning the Deity a gender. And then, as if to refute the notion of God the Mother, O'Neill lets Nina have her way: Nina the Dominatrix, the manipulator, the liar, the adulterer, the covetous and the spiteful. Jackson . . . is one of those rare performers whose presence is transfixing no matter what she does. While the entire cast is commendable, Ken Howard is especially wonderful and Edward Petherbridge is perfect as the cynical, effete, and yet ultimately loveable Charlie. But the real star is, of course, O'Neill's writing. Despite his pessimism and his convictions about the ugliness of life, his writing is the proof and affirmation of all that his miserable characters try to deny.
John Haslett Cuff, *Toronto Globe and Mail*, 16 Jan. 1988

Dynamo

Written: 1927-28.
First performed: Martin Beck Th., New York, 11 Feb. 1929 (dir. Philip Moeller; with Glenn Anders as Reuben Light, Dudley Digges as Ramsay Fife, and Claudette Colbert as Ada).
Published: revision of performance text, *Dynamo* (New York: Horace Liveright, 1929), in *Plays III*; in *Complete Plays 1920—1931*.

It is the probable intention of Mr. O'Neill's *Dynamo* to demolish not only the Old Time Religion but its substitutes, atheism and science, as answers to the riddle of this atom of the universe. As seen by him, the three of them fail in their endeavors to unlock the secret, and he leaves us at 11.10 pm, as much in the dark as we were at 8.50. All of the popular solutions are futile in *Dynamo* from Holy Writ to electricity. The powerhouse is as unsatisfactory a source of knowledge, according to Mr. O'Neill, as is the fundamentalist chapel, or the bench of the fool who saith in his heart that there is no God. But, while further mystifying us in our gropings to find light from the drama, Mr. O'Neill makes *Dynamo* an astonishing play. It is sometimes ludicrous, frequently raving, often encumbered with laborious 'interludisms', and generally an entertainment for the rarer playgoer. . . . The son of the evangelist . . . is enflamed by the daughter of the scoffer. . . . He has been a moony fellow [who] turns upon God with startling blasphemies. . . .

Thereafter he follows electricity as his Master and gets a job in the village power-plant. Here, he thinks, is the real deity. . . . He kneels in fanatic prayers before its dynamos and utters frenzied shrieks of worship. Miss Colbert, in a leggy red dress, tries to distract his attention from the machinery to her own poetic person, and she succeeds in doing so in a scarlet interlude hidden by a virtuous curtain. When he realizes that he has been untrue to electricity he shoots her and then kills himself in as vivid an exhibit of electrocution as has been seen since New York journalism photographed the Sing-Sing finish of Mrs. Snyder.

Percy Hammond,
New York Herald Tribune, 12 Feb. 1929

Those few of us who looked with something less than ecstasy on *Strange Interlude* when it appeared on that long afternoon over a year ago, may find a little justification for our scepticism in Mr. O'Neill's latest drama *Dynamo*. . . . *Dynamo* gives the tip–off on *Strange Interlude* and *The Great God Brown*. They were just as bad as we thought they were. Now we know.

It takes a great deal of concentration on *The Emperor Jones* and *The Hairy Ape* to keep alive the thought that Mr. O'Neill is America's greatest dramatist. Of course, if he isn't, the question arises 'Who is then?' and we scurry right back to Mr. O'Neill with apologies. . . .

Robert Benchley, *Life*, 8 Mar. 1929

In a lengthy and lugubrious letter to George Jean Nathan, Mr. O'Neill's father confessor, the author of *Dynamo* . . . points out that his latest invention is 'a symbolic and factual biography of what is happening in a large section of the American soul'. We moderns, it seems, are groping, groping for something with which to 'comfort our fears of death'. In an effort to relieve our alleged anxiety, Mr. O'Neill is in process of bringing forth . . . a trilogy which will eventually include last night's

Dynamo, tomorrow's *Without Ending of Days*, and next week's *It Cannot Be Mad*. After *It Cannot Be Mad* everything will be dandy.

When the curtain rises at the Martin Beck Theatre you see the open faced houses of the Lights and Fifes. The Lights, quaint creatures, believe in the manly God of their fathers. The Fifes, supposedly atheistic, believe in a female god known as Electricity. . . . So it goes for two acts out of three. . . . Nothing crops up that your nephew at Exeter would not settle by asking 'What difference does it make whether you speak of God as God, Electricity, The First Cause, Big or Dynamo?' . . . Perhaps you get the impression that Mr. O'Neill's *Dynamo* irks me. It does. . . .

Robert Garland, *New York Telegram*, 12 Feb. 1929

Mourning Becomes Electra

'A Trilogy.'
Written: 1929-31.
First performed: Theatre Guild, Guild Th., New York, 26 Oct. 1931 (dir. Philip Moeller; des. Robert Edmond Jones; with Alla Nazimova as Christine, Alice Brady as Lavinia, and Earle Larrimore as Orin).
First London performance: Westminster Th., 19 Nov. 1937 (with Laura Cowie as Christine, Beatrix Lehmann as Lavinia, Reginald Tate as Brant, and Robert Harris as Orin).
Revived: Alvin Th., New York, 9 May 1932; Amerikai Electra, Nemzeti Színház, Budapest, 1937; Gate Th., Dublin, 25 Oct. 1938 (dir. Hilton Edwards; with Coralie Carmichael as Christine, Meriel Moore as Lavinia, and Christopher Casson as Orin); as *Le Deuil sied à Electre*, Montparnasse, Paris, 1947 (mise en scène, G. Baty); Julius Slowacki Th., Krakow, Poland, 30 June 1962; Old Vic Th., London, 2 Dec. 1961 (dir. Oliver Neville; des. Michael Annals; with Barbara Jefford as Lavinia, Sonia Dresdel as Christine, Stephen Moore as Orin, and William Sylvster as Brant); Circle in the Square-Joseph Levine Th., New York, 15 Nov. 1972 (dir. Theodore Mann; with Colleen Dewhurst as Christine); Th. des Quartiers d'Ivry, Paris (mise en scène, Stuart Seide); Zuidelijk Toneel Th. of Eindhoven, touring various Dutch and Belgian cities, Apr.-May 1989 (dir. Ivo van Hove); Citizens Th., Glascow, 5 Apr. 1991 (dir. Philip Prowse; with Georgina Hale, Glenda Jackson, and Gerald Murphy.).
Film and television: RKO, 1947 (dir. Dudley Nichols; with Katina Paxinou as Christine, Rosalind Russell as Lavinia, and Michael Redgrave as Orin). PBS-WNET TV, five-part series beginning 6 Dec. 1978 (dir. Nick Havinga; with Joan Hackett as Christine, Roberta Maxwell as Lavinia, Bruce Davidson as Orin, Joseph

Sommer as Ezra, Robert Blossom as Seth, and Jeffrey DeMunn as Adam).

Opera: by Marvin David Levy, with libretto by Henry Butler, Metropolitan Opera, Mar. 1967 (dir. Michael Cacoyannis).

Recording: Caedmon (dir. Michael Kahn; with Jane Alexander, Sada Thompson, Lee Richardson, Robert Stattel, and Gene Nye), LP TRS 345 c.

Published: Mourning Becomes Electra (New York: Horace Liveright, 1931); in *Plays II*; in *Complete Plays 1920—1931.*

Mourning Becomes Electra *follows the scheme of the Orestes-Electra legend which Aeschylus, Sophocles, and Euripides translated into drama in the days of Greek classicism. Like the doomed house of Atreus, this New England family of Civil War time is dripping with foul and unnatural murder. The mother murders the father. The son murders his mother's lover. The mother mercifully commits suicide. The daughter's malefic importunities drive the son to suicide. It is a family that simmers with hatred, suspicion, jealousy, and greed, and that is twisted by unnatural loves. Although Mr. O'Neill uses the Orestes legend as the scheme of his trilogy, it is his ambition to abandon the gods, whom the Greeks humbly invoked at the crises of the drama, and to interpret the whole legend in terms of modern psychology. From Royalty this story of vengeance comes down to the level of solid New England burghers. From divinity it comes into the sphere of truths that are known. There are no mysteries about the inverted relationships that set all these gaunt-minded people against one another, aside from the primary mystery of the ferocity of life. Students of the new psychology will find convenient labels to explain why the mother betrays her husband, why the daughter instinctively takes the father's side, why the son fears his father and clings to his mother, why the daughter gradually inherits the characteristics of her mother after the deaths of the parents, and why the son transfers his passion to his sister. . . .*

Using a Greek legend as his model, [O'Neill] has reared up a universal tragedy of tremendous stature — deep, dark, solid, uncompromising, and grim. It is heroically thought out and magnificently wrought in style and structure, and it is played by Alice Brady and Mme. Nazimova with consummate artistry and passion. Mr. O'Neill has written overwhelming dramas in the past. . . . But he has never before fulfilled himself so completely; he has never commanded his theme in all its variety and adumbrations with such superb strength, coolness and coherence. To this department, which ordinarily reserves its praise for the dead, *Mourning Becomes Electra* is Mr. O'Neill's masterpiece. . . .

Although Mr. O'Neill has been no slave to the classic origins of his tragedy, he has transmuted the same impersonal forces into the modern idiom, and the production, which has been brilliantly directed by Philip Moeller, gives you some of the stately spectacle of Greek classicism. Lavinia in a flowing black dress sitting majestically on the steps of Robert Edmond Jones's set of a New England mansion is an unforgettable and portentous picture. Captain Brant pacing the deck of his ship in the ringing silence of the night, the murdered Mannon lying on his bier in the deep shadows of his study, the entrances and exits of Christine and Lavinia through doors that open and close on death are scenes full of dramatic beauty.

Brooks Atkinson,
New York Times, 27 Oct. 1931

The revival of Eugene O'Neill's *Mourning Becomes Electra* (Old Vic) at a time when obsequies are being read over the corpse of modern tragedy recalls the ballad about the wake that grew so lively that the dead man climbed out of his coffin and joined in. . . . [O'Neill] is a grave embarrassment to critics. He couples the highest claims with gross verbal ineptitude; and his work is built not on 'themes' of the Shaw and Ibsen variety, but on the raw magma of human passion. His plays echo Milton's Satan, 'Simply the thing I am shall make me live', a statement before which criticism stands disarmed. . . .

The Mannon family are living under a curse; their house has been built 'in hate'. But one never discovers what rule has been broken, or what form expiation must take. . . . This is not something O'Neill could have corrected, for divine law does not exist in the world he is writing about; it consists solely of the characters involved and the only rule is that of their own natures. These are laid bare partly with the aid of orthodox psychological equipment: thus the unfortunate General Mannon, the crypto-Agamemnon, returns from the war to find himself simultaneously the focus for an Electra and an Oedipus complex — either of which might have done for him had not his wife got in first with the fatal potion. . . .

O'Neill approached the [Oresteian] theme that obsessed him above all others . . . not in the offence its characters had committed, but in the fact that they were damned. O'Neill is the dramatist of the closed situation; his characters may take to the sea or the jungle, but those that do are making a futile attempt to break away from the narrow room where they belong. For them the outer world is a dream; they can neither join it nor receive help from it; their only reality is the hell of one another's company. And love in this prison is the greatest horror of all, for it keeps them in a state of defenceless vulnerability and chains them inescapably together. O'Neill found the true setting for this tragic view of human relationships when he turned to direct autobiography in *Long Day's Journey into Night*. . . .

[*Electra*] remains a giant in more ways than one; one may resist it and dismiss it as a dated stunt, but in the end one gives in and admits to membership of the family in the darkened room.

Irving Wardle, *The Observer*, Nov. 1961

Who dares wins. At a time when the characteristic sound of the British theatre is of hatches being battened down, the Glascow Citizens has had the chutzpah to revive . . . *Mourning Becomes Electra* (1931). Whatever flaws you may find in O'Neill's concept, Philip Prowse's four-hour production . . . is an assured and breathtaking triumph: it is like being confronted with the Grand Canyon after weeks of tiptoeing round herbaceous borders. . . .

What lifts the trilogy way above South Fork or Warner Bros melodrama is O'Neill's ability to sculpt his play not just in words but in sound and light; and Mr. Prowse's masterly production has the strange quality of 'unreal reality' O'Neill was after. He has devised a brilliant set in which sky-aspiring white pillars suggest the portico of some stately New England mansion and in which embossed black doors imply the entrance to a family vault. . . .

Glenda Jackson, in one of her best ever performances, makes Christine a hard, cruel, glittering woman in whom mockery and passion fight for supremacy. You see this in her greetings to her returning husband and son: the former she encounters with a withering cry of 'Is it really you Ezra?' while the latter is met with an atavistic rapture.

Georgina Hale has an even harder task as Lavinia, in that she has to motor the play, which she rises to superbly: she spits out her words with the caustic dryness of a baby Bette Davis and glides round the house with the unblinking eeriness of Mrs. Danvers yet at the last relinquishes her one true hope of love with a memorable and poignant regret. Gerald Murphy also doubles marvellously as both Ezra and Orin Mannon. . . .

O'Neill may not be Aeschylus, but he links private pain to public experience and has that quality of emotional intensity that is the very stuff of dramatic poetry.

Michael Billington,
Manchester Guardian Weekly, 21 Apr. 1991

Ah, Wilderness!

Written: 1932.

First performed: Nixon Th., New York, 25 Sept. 1933 (dir. Philip
   Moeller; des. Robert Edmond Jones; with George M. Cohan as Nat
   Miller, Elisha Cook Jr. as Richard, Gene Lockhart as Sid, Marjorie
   Marquis as Essie, and Ruth Gilbert as Muriel).

First performance in British Isles: Gate Th., Dublin, 24 Mar. 1936 (with
   Fred Johnson as Nat Miller, Ann Penhallow as Essie, Cyril Cusack as
   Richard, Edward Lexy as Sid, and Clodagh Garrett as Muriel).

Revived: many times; Vígszínház, Budapest, 1934; Guild Th., New
   York, 2 Oct. 1941; Yvonne Arnaud Th., Guildford, June 1972; Long
   Wharf Th., New Haven, Conn., 1974-75; Haft Th., New York, June
   1983 (dir. John Stix; with Philip Bosco and Dody Goodman); Oregon
   Shakespeare Festival, Ashland, 1983 season; Long Wharf Th., trans.
   to Neil Simon Th., New York, June 1988 (dir. Arvin Brown; with
   Jason Robards and Colleen Dewhurst).

Film and television: MGM, 1935 (dir. Clarence Brown; with Lionel
   Barrymore as Nat, Wallace Beery as Sid, Eric Linden as Richard,
   Spring Byington as Essie, and Cecilia Parker as Muriel); musical
   version, as *Summer Holiday*, MGM, 1948 (dir. Rouben Mamoulian;
   with Mickey Rooney as Richard, Walter Huston as Nat, Frank
   Morgan as Sid, Selena Royle as Mrs. Miller, Agnes Moorhead as
   Lily, and Gloria de Haven as Muriel).

Stage musical, as *Take Me Along,* Sam Schubert Th., New York, 22 Oct.
   1959 (with Walter Pigeon, Una Merkel, Eileen Herlie, Robert Morse,
   Susan Luckey, and Jackie Gleason); American Conservatory Th.,
   San Francisco, 1978 (dir. Allen Fletcher); African-American version,
   Richard Allen Center at Manhattan Community College, New York,
   Mar. 1984, (dir. Geraldine Fitzgerald and Mike Malone; adapted
   C. T. Perkinson).

Recording: Caedmon (with Geraldine Fitzgerald as Esssie, Larry Gates
   as Nat, Tony Schwab as Richard, Stefan Gierasch as Sid, and Brenda
   Currin as Muriel), LP TRS 340 c.

Published: acting version, as *Ah, Wilderness! A Comedy of
   Recollections in Three Acts* (New York: Samuel French, 1933); *Ah,
   Wilderness!* (New York: Random House, 1933; in *Plays II*; in
   Complete Plays 1932-1943.

---

*What concerns [the Miller family] is the youthful fervour of
Richard, who is a senior in high school and a rebel. He reads
Swinburne, Shaw, Wilde, and Omar Khayyam, and his mother*

worries. He is an incipient anarchist; he hates capital and his father looks disturbed. He is also passionately in love with a neighbour's girl, and means to marry her. The scraps of Swinburne verse that he sends to her alarm her father who forces her to break with Richard in good, melodramatic style. Being young and arrogant, Richard runs amok to spite her, and gets tight in the presence of a painted lady. His father and mother are sure that the world has come to an end. But the damsel manages to prove her devotion at a moonlit rendezvous on the beach and Richard is himself again. . . .

As a writer of comedy Mr. O'Neill has a capacity for tenderness that most of us never suspected. *Ah, Wilderness!* with which the Guild opened its sixteenth season last evening, may not be his most tremendous play, but it is certainly his most attractive.

As a Connecticut father of the year 1906, Mr. Cohan gives the ripest performance in his career, suggesting, as in the case of Mr. O'Neill, that his past achievements are no touchstone of the qualities he has never exploited. On the whole, Mr. O'Neill's excursion into nostalgic comedy has resulted in one of his best works. His sources are closer to life than the tortured characters of *Mourning Becomes Electra*. His mood is mature and forgiving. Now it is possible to sit down informally wth Mr. O'Neill and to like the people of whom he speaks and the gentle, kindly tolerance of his memories. . . .

The Guild has risen to the occasion nobly. Mr. Moeller's direction is supple, alert, and sagacious; and Robert Edmond Jones's settings recognize the humour in the stuffy refinement of 1906. As Nat Miller, the father, Mr. Cohan gives a splendid performance. . . . He is quizzical in the style to which we are all accustomed from him, but the jaunty mannerisms and the mugging have disappeared. . . . It has taken Eugene O'Neill to show us how fine an actor George M. Cohan is.

Brooks Atkinson, *New York Times*, 3 Oct. 1933

[O'Neill] has improved immensely in the present play over his immediately previous efforts — he has, in fact, almost reached the ability that he displayed when he first began writing — but the defect is still there. He spins out interminably situations that should have been touched on; he is painfully explicit concerning items that he should merely suggest; his motivation of mere stage mechanics — getting people on and off and the rest — is amazingly awkward. But then, it must be hard to get out of the marathon habits of *Interlude* and *Electra*; it is too much to expect that Mr. O'Neill could climb back to competence in one try.

Mainly it is the fault of the pitiful attempts at comedy, some of which, like the trite and obvious dinner-table-drunk scene, are merely cheap, and some of which, like the tasteless and horrible attempt to draw humour out of a sensitive lad getting drunk in a brothel, are frankly nauseating. . . .

[In the last scenes] Father Nat tries to tell [Richard] the facts of a certain part of life in a bungled, embarrassed, heart-moving way, and in the end young Richard goes out on the porch to sit in the moonlight, while his father and mother, arm in arm, climb upstairs to bed. Those last two scenes are sensitive and beautiful and tremendously effective; they are the first thing that we have had to remind us of the earlier and finer O'Neill. . . . A definitely promising play.

Eugene Burr, *Billboard*, 14 Oct. 1933.

Days without End

'A Modern Miracle Play.'
Written: 1931-33.
First performed: Plymouth Th., Boston, 27 Dec. 1933, trans. to Henry Miller Th., New York, 8 Jan. 1934 (dir. Philip Moeller; des. Lee Simonson; with Earle Larimore as John, Stanley Ridges as Loving, Robert Loraine as Father Baird, and Ilka Chase as Lucy).
First performance in British Isles: Abbey Th., Dublin, 16 Apr. 1934 (dir. Lennox Robinson; with F. J. McCormick, Arthur Shields, and Eileen Crowe).
Published: Days Without End: a Modern Miracle Play (Random House, 1934; in *Plays III*; *Complete Plays 1932-1943*.

O'Neill returns to a mixture of the *Strange Interlude* technique and the mask business of *The Great God Brown*. This Evil Spirit or 'Damned Soul' of John Loving is embodied on the stage by Stanley Ridges, hideously made up for grotesque effect, who never leaves Mr. Larimore's presence. He is the personification of the aside. He speaks the lines sometimes for John Loving; sometimes Mr. Larimore speaks them. When John Loving is in the throes of spiritual agony their dialogue monkeyshines become a joint debate between the Gold Dust Twins. . . . It is the devil that is finally cast out at the end, through the intercession of a priest, and Loving returns triumphantly to his old faith. . . . There is the intimation that Mrs. Loving will get well and that God is Love.

John Anderson, *New York Evening Journal*, 9 Jan. 1934

A Touch of the Poet

Written: 1935-42.

First performed: trans. Sven Barthel, Royal Dramatic Th., Stockholm, 29 Mar. 1957 (dir. Olof Molander; with Eva Dahlbeck as Sara, Sif Ruud, as Nora, Lars Hanson as Con, and Inga Tidblat as Deborah).

First American performance: Helen Hayes Th., New York, 2 Oct. 1958 (dir. Harold Clurman; with Kim Stanley as Sara, Helen Hayes as Nora, Eric Portman as Con, and Betty Field as Deborah).

First performance in British Isles: Olympia Th., Dublin, 24 Sept. 1962, trans. to Cambridge Arts Th., 8 Oct. 1962 (dir. Tony Robertson; des. Hutchinson Scott; with Ian Bannen, Billie Whitelaw as Sara, and Peggy Marshall as Nora).

Revived: Ashcroft Th., Croydon, 16 Sept. 1963 (dir. Hugh Goldie); ANTA Th., New York, 2 May 1967; Helen Hayes Th., New York, Jan. 1978 (dir. Jose Quintero; with Jason Robards, Geraldine Fitzgerald, and Kathryn Walker); Young Vic, London, Feb. 1988, trans. to Haymarket Th., 10 Mar. (dir. David Thacker; with Rudi Davies as Sara, Vanessa Redgrave as Nora, Timothy Dalton as Con, and Amanda Boxer as Deborah); Jane Mallett Th., St. Lawrence Centre, Toronto, Sept. 1988 (dir. Malcolm Black).

Film and television: PBS TV, 1974.

Published: New Haven, Conn.: Yale University Press, 1957; in *Later Plays*; in *Complete Plays 1932-1943*.

Given Eugene O'Neill and a cast of superb actors, the effect on stage is electric. . . . O'Neill used to feel that his dramas seldom or never had the force on the stage that he had imagined when he wrote them. If he could have seen the stunning performance that Harold Clurman has directed, it is possible that for once he might have been satisfied. For the performance fits the play exactly. And the performance includes the sort of inspired group acting that our theatre is seldom able to provide.

A Touch of the Poet is the [third] play in the projected cycle of eleven plays that O'Neill was never able to finish. The cycle was to record 175 years in the life of an American family — 'A Tale of the Possessors Self-Dispossessed' being the over-all theme. *A Touch of the Poet* is set in a gloomy tavern near Boston in 1828, and it has some bearing on the assimilation of European ideas in the businesslike democracy of America. . . .

Brooks Atkinson, *New York Times*, 3 Oct. 1958

It may not be one of O'Neill's masterpieces. But it has a rich comic—melodramatic texture and it adumbrates the themes he was to return to in

The Iceman Cometh and *Long Day's Journey.* On the one hand, O'Neill argues, we need our illusions; and, although Con wakes up to reality when he is engaged in a bruising battle with the police that ruins the scarlet uniform he wore at the battle of Talavera, you feel he has lost some vital part of himself. But, confining the action to a single day, O'Neill also creates a memorable picture of a family locked together in love and hate. That hint of quasi-incestuous intensity is the one element missing in Mr. Thacker's production. . . .

Vanessa Redgrave is simply astonishing as his peasant-wife. In terms of lines, the part is not large. But Ms Redgrave has the sagging, unharnessed breasts, the red, rawboned hands, the chafed heels resting on scuffed old shoes of the woman whose toil sustains her husband's dreams. Above all, she unforgettably suggests a woman who is still passionately in love with this husk of a man. When he plans a dinner celebrating the Talavera anniversary and says of a guest that he will be placed at his right hand, Ms Redgrave pats the table in affirmation as if it were the right hand of God himself.

Michael Billington, *Manchester Guardian Weekly*, 14 Feb. 1988

More Stately Mansions

Written: 1936-39.

First performed: trans. Sven Barthel, abridged by Karl Ragnar Gierow, Royal Dramatic Th., Stockholm, 11 Sept. 1962, (dir. Stig Thorsslow; with Inga Tidblat as Deborah, Jarl Kulle as Simon, and Gunnel Brostrom as Sara).

First American performance: abridged by Jose Quintero, Ahmanson Th., Los Angeles, 12 Sept. 1967, trans. to Broadhurst Th., New York (dir. Jose Quintero; with Helen Craig as Nora, Ingrid Bergman as Deborah, Arthur Hill as Simon, and Colleen Dewhurst as Sara).

First London performance: Greenwich Th., Sept. 1974 (dir. David Giles; with Dorothy Reynolds replacing Elizabeth Bergner as Deborah, Gary Bond as Simon, and Frances Cuka as Sara).

Revived: John Player Th., Dublin Th. Festival, 5 Oct. 1976 (dir. Nora Lever; with James Caffrey, Britta Smith, and Ena May).

Recording: Caedmon (adapted and dir. Jose Quintero; with Ingrid Bergman, Arthur Hill, and Colleen Dewhurst), LP TRS 333c.

Published: 'shortened from the author's partly revised script by Karl Ragnar Gierow and edited by Donald Gallup', New Haven and London: Yale University Press, 1964; 'The Unexpurgated Edition', ed. Martha Bower, New York: Oxford University Press, 1988, and, with a few changes, in *Complete Plays 1932-1943.*

It shows the triangle of Simon Harford, his mother Deborah, with whom he lives out childhood sexual fantasies, and his wife Sara Melody, who increasingly fuses with Deborah in Simon's mind.

[The typescript of the play's third draft survived O'Neill's attempt to destroy material from the unfinished 'Cycle' of eleven plays, 'A Tale of Possessors Self-Dispossessed', and reposes in the Beinecke Library at Yale. *More Stately Mansions* would have been the fourth play, following *A Touch of the Poet*. The draft of *More Stately Mansions* consists of more than 300 pages, typed single-spaced, with many revisions in O'Neill's hand.]

Greenwich Theatre's new season gets off to a shaky start with a slimline version of Eugene O'Neill's incomplete, unrevised final [sic] play, *More Stately Mansions*. Unfortunately Elizabeth Bergner and the production parted company last Friday; and although Dorothy Reynolds has taken her place with consummate professionalism, nothing can disguise the fact that the play tackles a classic Freudian situation in the manner of a nineteenth-century mortgage melodrama. . . .

Psychologically, the play is not untruthful: as Eric Bentley said, it's rather like seeing the crime of Oedipus recounted by Oedipus himself rather than by Sophocles. And the process by which the wife is finally transformed into the mother has a grisly, uncomfortable power. . . .

Michael Billington,
The Guardian, Sept. 1974

The Iceman Cometh

Written: 1939.
First performed: Theatre Guild, Martin Beck Th., New York, 9 Oct. 1946 (dir. Eddie Dowling; with Dudley Digges as Hope, E. G. Marshall as Willie, Morton L. Stevens as Mosher, Al McGranery as McGloin, Carl Benton Reid as Larry, Tom Pedi as Rocky, Paul Crabtree as Parritt, John Marriott as Joe, Nicholas Joy as Cecil, Russell Collins as Jimmy, Leo Chalzel as Hugo, Ruth Gilbert as Pearl, Jeanne Cagney as Margie, Marcella Markham as Cora, and James E. Barton as Hickey).
First performance in British Isles: Gate Th., Dublin, 7 June 1948 (dir. P. J. O'Connor; with Alex Andrews as Hope, Vincent Ellis as Willie, Rory Kilkenny as Larry, Jimmy Keogh as Parritt, and Pat Nolan as Hickey).

First London performance: Arts Th., Feb. 1958 (dir. Peter Wood; with Jack MacGowran as Hope, Lee Montague as Rocky, Michael Bryant as Willie, Patrick Magee as Larry, Vivian Matlon as Parritt, and Ian Bannen as Hickey).

Revived: Circle in the Square, New York, 8 May 1956 (dir. Jose Quintero; with Farrell Pelly as Hope, Addison Powell as Willie, Conrad Bain as Larry, Peter Falk as Rocky, Larry Robinson as Parritt, and Jason Robards Jr. as Hickey); as *Le Marchand de glace est passe*, Th. de la Commune d'Aubervilliers, 1967 (mise en scène, G. Garran); Vígszínház, Budapest, 1971; RSC, Aldwych Th., 25 Ma,1976 (dir. Howard Davies; with Norman Rodway as Hope, Bob Hoskins as Rocky, Patrick Stewart as Larry, Kenneth Cranham as Parritt, and Alan Tilvern as Hickey); Cottesloe Th., 4 Mar. 1980 (dir. Bill Bryden; des. Hayden Griffen; with Tony Haygarth as Larry, Kevin McNally as Parritt, and Jack Shepherd as Hickey); Lunt-Fontanne Th., New York, Nov. 1985 (dir. Jose Quintero; with Jason Robards); Ashland Shakespeare Festival, Oregon, 1988.

Film and television: Telefilm Associates, 1961 (dir. Sidney Lumet; with Farrell Pelly as Hope, James Broderick as Willie, Tom Pedi as Rocky, Myron McCormick as Larry, Robert Redford as Parritt, and Jason Robards Jr. as Hickey); American Film Theatre, 1973 (dir. John Frankenheimer; with Frederic March as Hope, Robert Ryan as Larry, Jeff Bridges as Parritt, Bradford Dillman as Willie, Sorrell Booke as Hugo, Hildy Brooks as Margie, Nancy Juno Dawson as Pearl, Evans Evans as Cora, Martyn Green as Capt. Lewis, John McLiam as Jimmy, Moses Gunn as Joe, Stephen Pearlman as Chuck, Tom Pedi as Rocky, George Voskovec as Piet, and Lee Marvin as Hickey).

Recording: Caedmon (as American Film Theatre version, above, with about an hour of text cut from film restored), LP TRS 359 c.

Published: Random House, 1946; in *Plays III* (later editions); *Complete Plays 1932-1943*.

The Iceman Cometh, *presented by the House of O'Neill, the Theatre Guild, in an admirably directed production by Eddie Dowling has stirred Broadway from its daydreaming even as his hero Hickey stirs the bums in the backroom of Harry Hope's dump from their alcohol-ridden fancies. . . . The whole action of the play, such as it is, swings between the bar itself with its half-door on the street and the dingy backroom where, as the curtain rises, a dozen assorted drunks sit at round tables drinking and dreaming of that golden tomorrow which will see them restored once more to a living world. They are waiting for Hickey, a travelling salesman, who comes to them from time to time to live out a 'periodical', a fabulous bender in which they share his whiskey and listen to his jokes, particularly that one about his loving wife whom he has treated so badly but who is all right now because he left her safely at home in bed — 'with the iceman'. . . . He had left her that very morning safe in bed — 'with the iceman', Death. And then as Hickey tells the story of the woman he murdered for love he realizes with a sudden blinding flash that this too was illusion, that he had killed her because he hated her; he killed her and cursed her for her intolerable, overwhelming love. This last confession brings a final reversal. The murder and the cursing were madness. . . . Hickey was crazy all the time! His reform was a pipe dream too. [The bums] can go back to their old illusions, their whiskey, their dreams; they reach thirstily for their bottles. Only the boy Parritt, Larry, and Hickey himself are changed. Hickey gives himself up to the police for murder, Parritt commits suicide . . . and Larry the philosopher faces the fact that for him too death is the only answer. The cycle is complete. If this is life then indeed 'the best of all were never to be born'.*

Like Peer Gynt's onion, the story of *The Iceman* has its layers and layers of meaning. . . . The play is in a very special sense a summary of much of O'Neill's past writing. . . . Don Parritt, the boy rejected by his mother, haunted by the guilt of his betrayal of her, which is nothing less than matricide, recalls O'Neill's days of absorption in psychoanalysis while Larry the philosopher is the O'Neill who attempted a detachment and objectivity never native to him.

But it is through Hickey who has known the love that passeth understanding and has rejected it that we glimpse O'Neill's ultimate meaning. Blind, besotted, and misguided, man haunted by death lives by lies. . . . The greatest illusion of all is to believe that disillusionment — the unaided processes of the intellect — can solve man's dilemma. There is a force that, like the love that Hickey's wife bore him, is made of understanding and forgiveness. Man finds such love intolerable. . . . And so man denies, destroys and blasphemes such love, only in the end to find that this too will be forgiven.

The denizens of Hickey's world and of the world at large find a simple answer to Hickey's final revelation. The man is mad! Hamlet to the contrary notwithstanding, there is nothing more in heaven and earth than can be compassed in any current philosophy. Pass the bottle. Drink up. What the hell! It's a good play, brother, why bother. . . .

[The four and a half hour] length of *The Iceman* . . . permits an interesting orchestration of effects . . . an antiphonal development of themes.

Mr. Dowling and the Theatre Guild have gathered a fine cast which gives as integrated a performance as has been seen in many a long day on the New York stage. Robert Edmond Jones has managed the miracle of making visible and at the same time expressive a sordid environment which is essential to the play but would lose its power were it merely photographic. James Barton [as] Hickey . . . . acquits himself with vigor of a task that might conceivably be more subtly handled. . . .

The Iceman Cometh, in fact, has many of Mr. O'Neill's old faults as well as his distinguishing virtues — it shows his complete lack of humour, his sententiousness and sentimentality — but it is immensely rich and rewarding to the playgoer and serves the welcome purpose of stirring argument and contention in the theatre, as Mr. O'Neill has done all his life. . . .

Rosamond Gilder, *Theatre Arts*, Dec. 1946

Although it has its tragic moments of pity and terror, this is no great play, but a tangled, grubby, fearsome, and fearful tract from a sick playwright who has given up hope and consigned humanity to despair; or drink, or dreams — or death. Let him come out into the sunlight.

Elliot Norton, *Boston Post*, 13 Oct. 1946

Though O'Neill sounds superficially like a complete defeatist, by implication he affirms that life, even with lies and illusions, is worth living. Even in its most hopeless moments his drama breathes a poetic reaffirmation of man's struggle toward dignity.

Life, 28 Oct. 1946

It is hard to be objective about this melancholy, sardonic drama that pulls the rug out from under the whole structure of life. It seems, not like something written, but like something that is happening. . . . Although the narrative is sprawling, the acting is vibrant in every part. . . . In both the writing and acting, *The Iceman Cometh* is a mighty theatre work. O'Neill is a giant and Mr. Quintero is a remarkably gifted artist.

Brooks Atkinson, *New York Times*, 9 May 1956

[How did O'Neill] hold us in our seats through four hours and more of circular alcoholic conversation? By means of verbal magic? I think not. . . . If it isn't the language, then, is it the universality of the theme? Again, no. Most of the characters are special cases, confirmed alcoholics out of touch with any kind of reality that cannot be bottled. When Hickey, the reformed drunk, urges these red-eyed wet-brains to abandon their pipe-dreams and face the truth about themselves, we know that the cure will kill them; but we cannot relate this knowledge to our own lives as we can, for instance, when Gregers Werle strips Ekdal of his illusions in *The Wild Duck*. Many of us, like Ekdal, have a dark-room of the soul where we develop dreams that the light of day would obliterate. But very few of us actually live in the dark-room, so enslaved to our fantasies that we would rather have DTs than give them up.

No, what holds us about the play is the insight it gives us into O'Neill himself. It is a dramatized neurosis, with no holds barred, written in a vein of unsparing, implacable honesty. 'Speak, that I may see thee', said Ben Jonson; and when O'Neill speaks, he hides nothing. Instead of listening to a story, we are shaking hands with a man, and a man whose vision of life is as profoundly dark as any since Aeschylus. It is this autobiographical intensity that grips us throughout the longueurs of the narrative and the gawkiness (I had almost said Gorkiness) of the style. For O'Neill, a pipe-dream is not just one alternative to despair: it is the only alternative. His bar-room derelicts comfort and sustain one another as long as each tolerates the others' illusions. Once Hickey has removed the illusions, nothing remains but guilt and mutual accusation. One may not agree with O'Neill's conclusions, but one cannot escape the look in his eye which is as magnetic as the Ancient Mariner's. He speaks like a man who has touched bottom himself; for whom words like inferior no longer have meaning. He is one of the few writers who can enter, without condescension or contempt, the world of those whom the world has rejected.

The play demands and gets superb direction. Peter Wood's production is better in many respects than the New York version I saw and admired last spring [directed by Jose Quintero]. . . . Jack McGowran, pinch-faced and baggy-trousered, plays the tetchy proprietor with a weasel brilliance I have not seen since the heyday of F. J. McCormick. . . . Of the three central characters, Patrick Magee does not quite get the rock-sombre melancholy of Larry, the disgusted nihilist who has deserted anarchism for drink; but the other two are perfect — Vivian Matalon as a guilty young stool-pigeon, pathetically ripe for suicide, and Ian Bannen as Hickey, the manic salesman, driving his friends to destruction with the enthusiasm of a revivalist. . . .

Kenneth Tynan, *The Observer*, Feb. 1958

This superb play is subtly acted and powerfully produced at the Arts

Theatre Club . . . It doesn't seem at all long. I could cheerfully sit through it again, and indeed shall. It comes, too, at a remarkably right time to remind us how lucky present-day American dramatists are to have had this great bulldozing genius opening up the terrain for them. . . . It has taken the delayed impact of the H-bomb on our thinking and feeling to bring us to the state of mind which can accept its sombre rejection of optimism, of the whole long liberal fallacy of the inevitability of progress by self-improvement, which has been since the nineteenth century the driving force of our civilization. O'Neill, in this play, plants an image, like a time bomb, in the very foundations of this belief and we watch the effects of its explosion in slow motion. . . .

The light [Hickey] has seen is not the light of old-time revivalism, it is the light that blazes at the heart of the liberal fallacy, that there exist two opposites called 'reality' and 'illusion' and that the first is 'good', the second 'bad'. . . . The experiment in self-improvement is an appalling failure all round. But if you see this as simply a failure of will on the part of the weak, you will, I believe, have missed O'Neill's point. He is not showing us, as Ibsen was in *The Wild Duck* (and as Eliot has done in our time too), that there are some who cannot bear too much reality. His attack is directed at the whole reality-illusion concept of opposites. The one figure we admire is the lonely, stubborn, desperate Larry Slade, who alone stands out against Hickey's high pressure salesmanship . . . [who was once] an important figure in the Wobblies . . . .

These reality-mongers are in fact supreme pipedreamers, no less self–deceptive than any of the whisky-bums. The reality Larry has forced himself to face is something very different from the pipedreaming recommended alike by political enthusiasts and the devotees of analysis, something that neither Marx nor Freud have stopped to reckon with, something beyond futile hope and fashionable pessimism, a courage that refuses to be fooled by either.

It is something like this, grand in conception and grandly carried out, that lies at the heart of this fine play. It is large and it is human, and it makes the fashionable dustbin drama of today seem merely trivial. Humorous, tender and intensely real, it belongs to the great order. . . .

T. C. Worsley,
New Statesman, 8 Feb. 1958

Long Day's Journey into Night

Written: 1940-41.
First performed: Royal Dramatic Th., Stockholm, 2 Feb. 1956 (transl.
Sven Barthel; dir. Bengt Ekerot; with Lars Hanson as Tyrone, Inga

Tidblat as Mary, Ulf Palme as Jamie, Jarl Kulle as Edmund, and
Caterine Westerlund as Cathleen).

First American performance: Wilbur Th., Boston, 15 Oct. 1956, trans. to
Helen Hayes Th., New York, 7 Nov. 1956 (dir. Jose Quintero; with
Frederic March as Tyrone, Florence Eldridge as Mary, Jason
Robards Jr. as Jamie, Bradford Dillman as Edmund, and Katherine
Ross as Cathleen).

First London performance: Globe Th., 18 Sept. 1958 (dir. Jose
Quintero; with Anthony Quayle, Gwen Ffrangcon-Davies, Ian
Bannen, and Alan Bates).

Revived: Abbey at Queen's Th., Belfast, 4 May 1959 (dir. Frank
Dermody; with Philip O'Flynn, Ria Mooney, T.P. McKenna, and
Vincent Dowling); Th. Slaski, Katowice, Poland, 19 Feb. 1961;
Nemzeti Színház, Budapest, 1963; National Th. at New Th., London,
21 Dec. 1971 (dir. Michael Blakemore; with Laurence Olivier,
Constance Cummings, Denis Quilley, and Ronald Pickup);
Promenade Th., New York, Apr. 1971; as *Le Long voyage vers la
nuit*, Atelier, Paris, 1973; Brooklyn, 1976 (dir. Jason Robards, who
also played Tyrone; with Zoe Caldwell, Kevin Conway, and Michael
Moriarty); Schubert Th., Boston, 3 May 1977 (dir. Michael Kahn;
with Jose Ferrer, Kate Reid, and Len Cariou); Milwaukee Repertory
Th., Jan. 1977 (dir. Irene Lewis); Avon Stage, Stratford, Ontario,
12 Oct. 1980 (dir. Robin Phillips; with Jessica Tandy, William Hutt,
Graeme Campbell, and Brent Carver); New York Shakespeare
Festival Public Th., 18 Mar. 1981 (dir. Geraldine Fitzgerald; with
Earle Hyman, Gloria Foster, Al Freeman Jr., and Peter Francis-
James); Broadhurst Th., New York, 21 Apr. 1986, trans. to Th.
Royal, Haymarket, London, 4 Aug., and to Tel Aviv (dir. Jonathan
Miller; with Jack Lemmon, Bethel Leslie, Kevin Spacey, and Peter
Gallagher); Royal Dramatic Th., Stockholm, 16 Apr. 1988 (dir.
Ingmar Bergman; with Jarle Kulle as Tyrone, Bibi Andersson,
Thommy Bergren, and Peter Stormare); Renmin Th., Nanjing, China,
June 1988; Artists Repertory Th., Portland, Oregon, May, 1990 (with
Vanna O'Brien); Majestic Th., Brooklyn Academy of Music, 14 June
1991 (Royal Dramatic Th. of Stockholm production of 1988);
National Th. at the Lyttleton, 15 May 1991, preceded by a national
tour (dir. Howard Davies, with Timothy West as Tyrone, Prunella
Scales, Sean McGinley, and Stephen Dillane).

Film and television: 1962 (dir. Sidney Lumet; with Ralph Richardson as
Tyrone, Katherine Hepburn as Mary, Jason Robards as Jamie, Dean
Stockwell as Edmund, and Jeanne Barr as Cathleen); ITV, 22 Apr.
1973 (National Th. production with Olivier); PBS TV, 1981 (dir.
William Woodman; with Earle Hyman as Tyrone, Ruby Dee as
Mary, Peter Francis-James as Edmund, and Thommie Blackwell as

Jamie); PBS American Playhouse, 1986 (with Jack Lemmon, Bethel Leslie, Peter Gallagher, and Kevin Spacey), recording by Caedmon (with Robert Ryan as Tyrone, Geraldine Fitzgerald as Mary, Stacey Keach as Jamie, and James Naughton as Edmund), LP TRS 350 c.

Published: New Haven: Yale University Press, 1956; in *Complete Plays 1932-1943.*

Eugene O'Neill wrote this play in 1940. Since it is a painfully autobiographical work, he did not wish to have it published or performed until twenty-five years after his death. His wife, Carlotta Monterey O'Neill, to whom the play is touchingly dedicated, has consented to have it published here and performed in Sweden three years after his death. I believe she was right. Who knows what such a play — or any play — will mean twenty-five years after an author's death? At the present moment, the play is a precious gift to us — regardless of its ultimate value.

I say this, though on a first reading I cannot determine what I actually think of it as a work of art or simply as a play. I am moved and fascinated by it in a personal way. The fact that the Swedes were held by it and did not complain of its four and one-half hours of length indicates something about its theatrical viability. It is indisputable that O'Neill's plays are nearly always more impressive on the stage than on the printed page. I should very much like to see this play done on or off Broadway. If such a play is 'impractical' for our theatre, so much the worse for our theatre. The play is the testament of the most serious playwright our country has produced.

To say this is not to set oneself down as an unqualified O'Neill admirer. O'Neill was a faulty craftsman; he was not a sound thinker. Though he probably read more extensively and profoundly than most of our playwrights, O'Neill could not by any 'universal' standard be considered a cultivated man. His view of life is circumscribed, he is often raw, naive, sentimental, and pessimistic in a somewhat adolescent manner.

Yet to dwell on these shortcomings as if they negate the value of the man to our stage and to our culture is to confess one's own inadequate and bloodless response to the world we live in. For in a time and place where life is experienced either as a series of mechanistic jerks or sipped in polite doses of borrowed sophistication . . . O'Neill not only lived intensely but attempted with perilous honesty to contemplate, absorb, and digest the meaning of his life and ours. He possessed an uncompromising devotion to the task he set himself: to present and interpret in stage terms what he had lived through and thought about — devotion in our theatre. . . .

The father's confession leads to the boy's (the author's) own confession of what his youthful escapades at sea have meant to him: it is a dream of beatitude, a seeking for God and wholeness — as direct, unabashed, and truly soulful as any ever to be written by an American dramatist. To which his father replies, 'Yes, there's the makings of a poet in you all right', and O'Neill answers, 'The makings of a poet . . . I couldn't touch what I tried to tell you just now. I stammered. That's the best I'll ever do. . . . Well, it will be faithful realism at least.'

O'Neill's work is more than realism. And if it is stammering — it is still the most eloquent and significant stammer of the American theatre. We have not yet developed a cultivated speech that is either superior to it or as good.

Harold Clurman, on the published text,
The Nation, 3 Mar. 1956

Long Day's Journey into Night is not so much a play as a continuously absorbing exegesis of Mary Tyrone's line, 'The past is the present, isn't it? It's the future, too. We all try to lie out of that but life won't let us'. . . .

For those who are familiar with some of the details of O'Neill's tragic life and with the twenty-five full-length plays that gained him his reputation as America's greatest playwright, this merciless autobiography is enormously interesting. But even for those who are not, there is a breadth to [the play] that may make it the most universal piece of stage realism ever turned out by an American playwright. For doesn't it expose the forces that work both to unite and to tear asunder all human groups? . . .

Director Jose Quintero and a dedicated cast have done a remarkable job in performing the four-hour play with such inner concentration that we are seldom conscious of the time. Frederic March's James Tyrone is a miraculously sustained portrayal. He starts off as a man more or less resigned to the waywardness of his sons, but with cheerfulness maintained by the hope that his wife will not resume her narcotics habit; his narrow view of religion equates God and hope. Once she does resume Mr. March visibly resigns himself to going the rest of the way without faith. . . . As Mary, Florence Eldridge is at her best when she nervously goes on the defensive about her addiction or when she gets a mad look in her eye as she describes her wedding gown. There are times, however, when we would like to see more feeling toward her sons, and other times when we are not as aware as we should be that she is under the influence of drugs.

Mr. Quintero has directed the play with great fidelity, resisting the getting of a dramatic impact at the expense of the production's total truthfulness. He begins the long day with the family normal and jovial. . . .

Mr. Quintero makes no attempt to rush a grim tone into the proceedings. He allows the mutual recriminations to develop slowly and naturally. Thus, everything that ensues seems a part of life in the Tyrone summerhouse rather than scenes from a play. David Hayes's set is a beauty, changing character from day to night, and Tharon Musser's lighting is superb as it strengthens each important moment. . . .

Henry Hewes,
Saturday Review, 24 Nov. 1956

Eugene O'Neill died five years ago. The eclipse of reputation that commonly befalls great men as soon as they die has not yet happened to him; and now that *Long Day's Journey into Night* has followed *The Iceman Cometh* into London I doubt if it ever will. . . . [O'Neill's strength] has nothing to do with intellect, verbal beauty, or the accepted definitions of tragedy and comedy. It exists independently of them: indeed they might even have cramped and depleted it.

What is this strength, this durable virtue? I got the clue to it from the American reviewer Stark Young . . . [who wrote in 1926] 'what moved us was *the cost to the dramatist* of what he handled' (my italics). Two years later, reviewing *Dynamo*, he developed this idea. He found in the play an 'individual poignancy' to which he responded no matter how tritely or unevenly expressed. From this it was a short step to the truth. 'Even when we are not at all touched by the feeling itself or the idea presented', he wrote, 'we are stabbed to our depths by the importance of this feeling to him, and we are all his, not because of what he says but because saying it meant so much to him.'

Thirty years later, we are stabbed in the same way, and for the same reason. The writing of *Long Day's Journey* must have cost O'Neill more than Mr. Young could ever have conceived . . . . The London production is much shorter than those I saw in Berlin and New York: about a quarter of the text has been cut away. This is shrewd pruning, since a non-American-English-speaking cast might not have been able to sustain the full four-hour burden. Alan Bates, shock-haired and forlorn, approaches Edmund with just the right abandon: once inside the part, however, he stumbles over a distracting North-country accent. Ian Bannen, on the other hand, gets easily to the heart of the elder brother, especially in the last-act debauch when he confesses to Edmund how much he hates and envies him: what he misses is the exterior of the seedy Broadway masher. He falls short of his New York counterpart, Jason Robards, just as far as Anthony Quayle falls short of Frederic March. Mr. March, with his corrugated face and burning eyes, looked as weighty as if he were made of iron. Mr. Quayle, though he conveys every syllable of the part's meaning, never seems to be heavier than tin.

By West End standards, let me add, all these performances are exceptionally good. That of Gwen Ffrangcon-Davies is by any standards magnificent. In this production Mother is the central figure: a guileful, silver-topped doll, her hands clenched by rheumatism into claws, her voice drooping except when drugs tighten it into a tingling, bird-like tightrope brightness. Her sons stare at her and she knows why they are staring, but: 'Is my hair coming down?' she pipes, warding off the truth with a defence of flirtation. At the end, when the men are slumped in a stupor, she tells us in a delicate quaver how the whole mess began. 'Then I married James Tyrone, and I was happy for a time. . . .' The curtain falls on a stupendous evening. One goes expecting to hear a playwright, and one meets a man.

Kenneth Tynan,
The Observer, 28 Sept. 1958

It is difficult to imagine a better cast than the one assembled at the New. As James Tyrone Laurence Olivier gives what will surely be remembered as one of his great performances. There is something particularly moving in watching him enter the skin of an actor who, unlike himself, sold out by playing the easy role of Count of Monte Cristo for years until he realized, too late, that he had gambled away his talent. Despite an abundance of familiar Olivier tricks — the balancing act on the table; the rolling Shakespearian quotations — what is remarkable about his Tyrone is its totality: the bullish selfishness; the flashes of Irish flair; the moments of tenderness; and then despair, setting hard across his shoulders. Olivier plays him as a still-robust man, with age approaching in the slackening of jaw muscles and in the dull hopelessness of his eyes, as they will his wife the strength to resist a return to drugs. It's a performance of immaculate detail, and the magnificent drunken speech in the last act, when he admits his life-long obsessive dread of the poorhouse . . . is delivered with breathtaking range, his whole body echoing the strain of the confession.

As Edmund, Ronald Pickup is able, for the first time, fully to release his potential. This, too, is a striking physical performance: the tics in his gaunt cheeks reflecting the suffering caused as his mother blames her addiction on his birth, her present condition on his illness; the large, dark eyes showing fear and love at her equally inevitable apologies. Yet, behind the vulnerability, he indicates that here, in other circumstances, is a young man of irrepressible energy. Pickup completely avoids the pitfall of self-pity and, especially in the massive final scenes with his father and brother, reveals a rare ability for restrained, but dramatic reaction. . . .

Helen Dawson, *The Observer*, 2 Feb. 1972

One could have foretold that Sidney Lumet's version of O'Neill's *Long Day's Journey into Night* would have a rough ride with the dogmatists of cinema theory . . . [but it] seems to be a good film because Lumet has understood and lit up a courageous, roaring, harrowing text, and if anything I think it works more truly in this form than in the theatre, even if it is nearly two hours shorter than the gigantic original.

The text seems to have been gouged out of O'Neill's gut. Lumet directs the characters so that their accusations are often more softly spoken than their apologies, as though they wanted to draw the sting. They are trapped in a kind of love that is nothing but bondage, and none of them are free to admit that when they are angry they are likely to be saying things that they profoundly mean; they hope they aren't true, that the feelings will pass soon. This is where Lumet has photographed the play so beautifully. The film edited so that the suspicions and misgivings on their faces flicker through the text as eloquently as a second language. I doubt if the peculiar stammering candour of O'Neill has ever been better served, even if half those old devil words have had to go down the sink.

Penelope Gilliatt,
The Observer, 1962

Hughie

Written: 1941.

First performed: with Strindberg's *The Stronger*, Royal Dramatic Th., Stockholm, 18 Sep. 1958, (transl.ated by Sven Barthel; dir. Bengt Ekerot; with Bengt Eklund as Erie, and Alan Edwall as Charlie).

First London performance: Duchess Th., 10 June 1963 (dir. Alfred Allan Lewis; with Burgess Meredith and Jack MacGowran).

First American performance: Royale Th., New York, 22 Dec. 1964 (dir. Jose Quintero; with Jason Robards and Jack Dodson).

Revived: Irodalmi Színpad, Budapest, 1965; Eblana Th., Dublin, Oct. 1966 (dir. Sean Cotter); John Golden Th., New York, 18 Feb. 1975 (dir. Martin Fried; with Ben Gazzarra); numerous American revivals since about 1976, including several with Jason Robards and Jack Dodson; National Th. at the Cottesloe, London, Jan. 1980 (dir. Hayden Griffith; with Stacy Keach).

Film and television: RKO-Nederlander, 1981 (dir. Jose Quintero and Terry Hughes; with Jason Robards and Jack Dodson).

Published: New Haven: Yale University Press, 1959); in *Later Plays*; *Complete Plays 1932-1943*.

[Hughie] was the night clerk in a seedy West Side hotel where all the action takes place. He has only recently died, we gather, and his job has been taken by another dim little man who, in the intervals of registering the dumbest courtesies to the hotel's guests, dreams of being a garbage collector, crashing dustbins around, a fireman at the great fire that would burn the city to the ground. He is nodding under his light bulb when 'Erie' Smith appears, namely Mr. Jason Robards got up in a stained panama suit, a sleazy tie, and the all too brief authority of a gambler, gangster's runner, and racing tout who struts, winks, declaims about his gaudy days because quite plainly they will come no more. . . .

Some of the critics have been complaining that *Hughie* is a mere cartoon for what O'Neill in his prime would have turned into a huge and overwhelming canvas. No doubt he would. But the joy of *Hughie* is to see an O'Neill play written with blessed restraint, saying what must be said, and no more, in seventy minutes. And the special joy of the first night was to see Jason Robards sensing through his nerve ends that this was not a sketch but a late masterpiece, which he is totally equipped to perform.

Alistaire Cooke,
Manchester Guardian Weekly, 31 Dec. 1964

O'Neill in *Hughie* has written the whole cycle of life into a forty-minute piece. The wise guy and the sucker stand for all forms of human interdependence. The swing from naked truth to illusion, from isolation to communication, from bitterness to love, are all basic to living. We alternate from one to the other, and this cyclic motion rather than the achievement of a goal is the stuff and richness of life. . . .

Mr. Eklund plays Erie less as a cheap Broadway sharpie than as a crumpled victim of life's racket. It is an understated performances which sacrifices something in explosiveness and fire to bring credibility to a play whose denouement might otherwise seem too mechanical. And its finest moments come between lines when Erie and the night clerk suddenly realize their isolation from each other.

For O'Neill, who wrote this perfectly constructed work at about the same time as *A Moon for the Misbegotten*, as the first in a never-completed series of short plays to be entitled 'By Way of Obit', had come to believe that the interdependence of human beings, even when it is selfishly motivated, contains a divine element of love.

Henry Hewes,
Saturday Review, 4 Oct. 1958

Five days ago Hughie was buried. Erie spent a hundred bucks on a floral tribute — a giant horseshoe of roses and forget-me-nots — and then went on a bender. It was a hundred bucks Erie did not have, and his gambling has since been disastrous. Tomorrow maybe, or the day after, the boys are going to come around to beat him up for nonpayment of dues.

Erie talks, and as he talks his need for Hughie spills out. Hughie was the man who made Erie feel the way Erie felt he ought to feel. Nor was this a one-way transaction — such permanent emotional arrangements rarely are — for clearly Hughie also got another view of himself from the relationship. It was a kind of love.

O'Neill is always the poet of the prosaic, you feel the sharp pain of his characters, as well as their gritty gallantry, because they are all images of the playwright himself, his imagination is stained with his life's blood.

When *Hughie* was first staged on Broadway, at the end of 1964 with Jason Robards, it was coolly received. It should not be on this occasion. Do not underrate its garrulous pungency. It is also beautifully played by [Ben] Gazzarra and Peter Maloney as the night clerk. Gazzarra, with his indelible grin, sadly creased face, and air of punch-drunk confidence, shadow-boxing deftly with his past, present, and future, is a joy to watch. He is playing a real man who has elected to make a caricature out of himself, his toughness is as vulnerable as papier-mache, yet still has the reality of its own illusion. . . .

Clive Barnes, *New York Times*, 19 Feb. 1975

Stacy Keach's Erie cannot be faulted except for its carefulness; you expect a visiting American star to be a bigger spender. . . .

Robert Cushman,
The Observer, 27 Jan. 1980

A Moon for the Misbegotten

Written: 1941-43.

First performed: Theatre Guild, Hartman Th., Columbus, Ohio, 20 Feb. 1947 (dir. Arthur Shields; with Mary Welch as Josie, J. M. Kerrigan as Hogan, and James Dunn as Jim), followed by tour.

First performance in Bitish Isles: Belfast Arts Th., Northern Ireland, 6 Apr. 1954; trans. to Dublin Gas Co. Th., 19 Apr. (dir. Hubert R. Wilmot; with Susan Lyde, Terence Pim as Phil, and Bryn Bartlett as Jim).

Revived: Bijou Th., New York, 2 May 1957 (dir. Carmen Capalbo, with Wendy Hiller, Cyril Cusack, and Franchot Tone); Arts Th., London, Jan. 1960 (dir. Clifford Williams; with Margaret Whiting as Josie, Colin Blakely as Hogan, and Michael Aldridge as Tyrone); Circle in the Square, New York, 12 June 1968 (dir. Theodore Mann; with Salome Jens, W. B. Brydon, and Mitchell Ryan); as *Une Lune pour les desherites*, Th. Club des Nantes, 1971; Odéon, 1973 (mise en scène, J. Rosner); Spoleto Festival of Two Worlds, Italy, 1973 (dir. Jose Quintero; with Colleen Dewhurst, Farrell Pelly, and Richard Kiley); Morosco Th., New York, 29 Dec. 1973 (dir. Jose Quintero; with Colleen Dewhurst and Jason Robards Jr.); Riverside Studios, Hammersmith, June, 1983 (dir. David Leveaux; with Frances de la Tour, Alan Devlin as Hogan, and Ian Bannen as Tyrone); Maison des Arts Andre Malraux, 1984 (mise en scène, L. Fevrier); Abbey Th. Co. from Dublin at Spaulding Auditorium, Dartmouth College, Hanover, New Hampshire, 27 Mar., 1990 (dir. Vincent Dowling; with David Kelly as Phil, Britta Smith as Josie, and Bosco Hogan as Jim Tyrone); Conservatory, Vancouver, Nov. 1990 (dir. Nick Tattersall; with Lee Van Passen as Josie); Williamstown Th. Festival, Massachusetts, 1990 (dir. Kevin Dowling; with Pat Hingle as Hogan, Christine Lahti as Josie, and Jamey Sheridan as Jim).

Film and television: ABC-TV, 1975 (dir. Jose Quintero and Gordon Rigsby; with Colleen Dewhurst, Ed Flanders, and Jason Robards).

Published: Random House, 1952; in *Later Plays*; *Complete Plays 1932-1943*.

Down on the farm in old Connecticut a melodrama is on the boil. Rich landlord plans to evict poor old man and daughter; miserable sinner craves for the love of pure woman; tyrannical father bares a heart of gold; local trollop reveals that she's a virgin in disguise. That is the corny framework of A Moon for the Misbegotten, *whose clumsy plot is plastered with laborious rustic repartee and self-conscious poeticizing. Most of it is written in a strong Irish brogue at the top of the author's voice. But the author is Eugene O'Neill, and the voice that breaks through cries out at times with a savage, blistering intensity of communicated feeling which, burning away the melodramatic surround, makes the kind of immediate living connection with here-and-now experience for which you may wait in vain through scores of current critical pops. . . .*

Richard Findlater, *Encore*, Apr. 1960

A Moon for the Misbegotten is another of Eugene O'Neill's dark and brooding contemplations of tormented souls. The last work of our great dramatist, it suffers from his characteristic failings of excessive length and insufficient eloquence, but, whatever its incidental weaknesses may be, it is a moving, beautiful, and shattering play. Admirably enacted by Wendy Hiller, Franchot Tone and Cyric Cusack, its first local performance at the Bijou Theater last night was a haunting emotional experience and one of the memorable events of recent theatrical seasons.

It is a remarkable tribute to a playwright when the only possible current rivals to one of his dramas are a couple of his other works, and *A Moon for the Misbegotten* must inescapably be compared to *Long Day's Journey into Night* and *The Iceman Cometh*. There is no way of avoiding, or reason for denying, that his final play is the least satisfying of the three. In it, their faults unquestionably bulk larger. But this has little to do with the fact that, after *A Moon for the Misbegotten* has managed its occasionally tedious beginning, it is overwhelming. . . .

Wendy Hiller, who plays the girl, may not meet O'Neill's demands for physical bulk in the role, but she plays so beautifully that this becomes unimportant. Years after he deserved to be, Franchot Tone has come to be accepted as one of the ablest of American actors, but he has never been so brilliant as he is in the magnificent part of the lost alcoholic. And Cyril Cusack, one of the most talented of contemporary Irish actors, is splendid as the father. *A Moon for the Misbegotten* is further proof that Eugene O'Neill was one of the Titans of the theatre.

Richard Watts, New York Post, 3 May 1957

Mr. O'Neill, who had written the dimensions for his leading lady, then proceeded to overlook his own measurements. 'That doesn't matter to me', he retorted. 'She can gain some more weight, but the important thing is that Miss Welch understands how Josie feels. These other girls, who are closer physically to Josie, somehow don't know how tortured she is, or can't project it. The inner state of Josie is what I want. We'll work the other problems out in clothes and sets.'

Mary Welch, 'Softer Tones for Mr. O'Neill's Portrait',
Theatre Arts, May 1957,
on being cast as the first Josie Hogan

I believe Jason Robards was miscast [as Jim Tyrone] and, after seeing the Guthrie production, I believe I can explain why. . . . The simple truth of Nick Havinga's faithful direction is that James Tyrone Jr. is not the most important character in *Moon*. He is not even the second most important character; Josie's father is. . . . [The Tyrone at the Guthrie,

Peter Michael] Goetz delivered Jim's major confessional speech in Act III in the manner O'Neill calls for — 'His voice becomes impersonal and objective, as though what he told concerned some man he had known, but had nothing to do with him.' . . . To deliver Jamie's confession as Robards did, in a manner suitable to Hickey's confession in *Iceman*, is to force *A Moon* to appear as misshapen in performance as it does when read through an autobiographical screen. . . . When [Jordan Y.] Miller writes that 'We have little interest in James Tyrone Jr. himself, a petty figure, whose maudlin confession of his sins creates only disgust and revulsion', he is very close to the truth. We are neither supposed nor allowed to be that interested in Jim Tyrone because he is not the focal point; Josie is.

Paul D. Voelker,
Eugene O'Neill Newsletter, Jan. 1978

[The success of] *A Moon for the Misbegotten* is . . . dependent on quality of performance. David Leveaux's splendid production at Riverside Studios justifies O'Neill's renewed faith in the power of actors to solve dramatic problems. . . .

Frances de la Tour's Josie is a work of genius. Colleen Dewhurst's muscular performance in the 1974 New York revival, full of rasp and perspiration, cannot match the skilful blend of awkwardness and elegance which de la Tour brings to this difficult role. If she lacks the imposing physicality so often the target of Phil Hogan's jeers — O'Neill says 'she is so oversize for a woman that she is nearly a freak' — then her intensity and range more than compensate. Without losing her grasp on the character's essential nature, she permits us to see Josie through Jim's eyes; no mean accomplishment considering the chameleonic talent which that requires. . . .

Other members of the company are also impressive. Ian Bannen's Jim seems at first more Wall Street than Broadway, but he quickly shakes off his broker's stiffness and acquits himself commendably. Few celebrated playwrights need to be saved from themselves as much as O'Neill, but where rescue is necessary . . . Bannen's choices are almost always right. David Leveaux must be congratulated for directing at a refreshingly varied pace which respects the play's humour as well as its lyricism.

David Hirson,
Times Literary Supplement, 15 July 1983

[In the Abbey Theatre production of 1990, the action up to Jim's return to the farm late in Act II] is a clear invitation to sit back and enjoy the most popular kind of comic theatre. In this action, the engineer and chief actor is Phil Hogan, with Jim as straight man and Josie as audience. . . . [David] Kelly's Phil is masterful; he holds the first half of the play together with his versatile and vastly entertaining histrionics.

If the second half of the play is somewhat less successfully brought off in this production, it is not from any lack of understanding of its implications. That Phil's entrapment scheme is literally drowned out by the story of Jim's suffering is amply communicated in the third act. Bosco Hogan's Jim Tyrone is correctly one who is physically and psychologically at the end of his rope, but who never appears to others to be as drunk as he invariably is. Mr. Hogan also lets the early intimations that Jim Tyrone is haunted by some terrible memory gradually envelop his personality in the third act, little by little replacing infectious wit as the play progresses.

And Britta Smith's Josie really stands out in these scenes. The Abbey was fortunate to have her available for the role. Her facial expressions, shifting vocal tones and bodily movements convincingly reveal Josie's struggle to remember that she is supposed to be seducing Jim, not loving him, and to hide the fact that beneath the 'smut stuff' she 'is a virgin'. It is not only her ample but firm dimensions that are entirely appropriate to Josie, but also the direct simplicity of her gaze and the authenticity of a warmth and gentleness which enable her to hold the 'dead child' Jim in her arms for half a night. O'Neill's Josie naturally speaks in clichés, so the challenge to the actress playing her is to reveal the truths underlying the cliches. Smith achieves this wonderfully. It would be regrettable if more American audiences did not have opportunity to see her play the role in the future.

Why, then, is the second half less successfully brought off? . . . It is hard to accept Mr. Hogan's going through Jim's entire third-act confession (regarding his behaviour following his mother's death) from a seated position. His body in motion must be as much a part of his gargantuan guilt in these moments as what he says. Dowling and Bosco Hogan did surprisingly little with body movements here, despite all that was achieved histrionically in conveying Jim's remarkable mixture of personal characteristics elsewhere. The Sophoclean dimensions of Jim's great confessional speech, as delivered by Bosco Hogan, was more an intellectual than an emotional experience (which may, of course, have been a relief to some in the audience). But if Hogan's Jim never reaches us as a suffering Christ, which O'Neill appears to want by creating the Pieta image at the close of the third act, Britta Smith's Josie certainly does reach us as Virgin Mother. And this play, finally, is not so much about guilt as forgiveness. . . .

Michael Manheim,
Eugene O'Neill Review, Spring-Fall 1990

Throughout his life O'Neill wrote occasional poems, more frequently between 1912 and 1919 Of these, 62 are collected by Donald Gallup in *Eugene O'Neill's Poems 1912-1944*. Several early poems appeared in the *Telegraph* of New London, Connecticut, during O'Neill's stint as a feature writer. Dr. Gallup prints three poems written in Bermuda in 1925, and seven more poems written between 1940 and 1944. Dr. Gallup has also transcribed *Eugene O'Neill Work Diaries 1924-1943*, which are of great interest.

O'Neill wrote a few short stories including one (destroyed) he called 'The Hairy Ape,' about a stoker named Driscoll he had known at sea and in New York, and another called 'Tomorrow' about James Findlater Byth, the model for Jimmy Tomorrow in *The Iceman Cometh*, who had saved O'Neill's life in 1912, and who killed himself a year and a half later; the story was published in *The Smart Set*, June, 1917, and is reprinted in *Complete Plays 1932-1943*.

O'Neill, a prolific correspondent, wrote forthright, profane, funny, and memorable letters. In addition to a general collection, edited by Travis Bogard and Jackson Bryer, *Selected Letters of Eugene O'Neill*, there are also special collections of his correspondence with notable friends, including Kenneth MacGowan, in *The Theatre We Worked For*, edited by Jackson R. Bryer with Ruth M. Alvarez; with George Jean Nathan, in *As Ever, Gene*, edited by Nancy L. Roberts and Arthur W. Roberts; and with Saxe Commins, in *Love and Admiration and Respect*, edited by Dorothy Commins.

I rate myself as a beginner — with prospects. I acknowledge that when you write: 'He sees life too often as drama. The great dramatist is the dramatist who sees drama as life', you are smiting the nail on the head. But I venture to promise that this will be less true with each succeeding play — that I will not 'stay put' in any comfortable niche and play the leave-well-enough-alone game. God stiffen it, I am young yet and I mean to grow! . . .

In the Zone — your [phrase] 'vaudeville grand guignolism' is my own verdict — but I am out of that zone now, never to return. As for *The Rope*, I do believe that is sound enough, although it's a year or more since I looked at it and perhaps I'd agree with you now. But where did you get the idea that I really valued *Where the Cross Was Made*? It was great fun to write, theatrically very thrilling, an amusing experiment in treating the audience as insane — that is all it means or ever meant to me.

> Letter to George Jean Nathan, 20 Jun. 1920,
> answering Nathan's praise and criticism in
> 'The American Playwright,' *Smart Set*, July 1920

My direst grudge against *Monte Cristo* is that, in my opinion, it wrecked my father's chance to become one of our greatest actors. Since he did not mince this matter himself but confessed it to me during our very close 'palship' last winter, I feel free to state it. *Monte Cristo*, he often said with great bitterness as he lived over his past out loud to me, had been his curse. He had fallen for the lure of easy popularity and easy money — and he suffered as a retribution in his old age the humiliation of supporting such actor-yokels (by comparison) as Tynan, Allen, Fredericks, Elliott, etc. How keenly he felt this in the last years, I think I am the only one who knows, the only one he confided in. He felt also that he had made a bad bargain. The money was thrown away, squandered in wild speculations, lost. He was leaving my Mother with the barest sufficiency. Even now, she is having difficulty in getting his messed-up estate into a sane condition where it can maintain her with a fair degree of comfort. The treasures of *Monte Cristo* are buried deep again — in prairie dog gold mines, in unlubricated oil wells, in fuelless coal lands — the modern Castles in Spain of pure romance.

My father died broken, unhappy, intensely bitter, feeling that life was 'a damned hard billet to chew'. His last words to me — when speech had almost failed him — were: 'Eugene — I'm going to a better sort of life. This sort of life — here — all froth — no good — rottenness!' This after seventy-six years of what the mob undoubtedly regard as a highly successful career! It furnishes food for thought, what? I have quoted his words verbatim. They are written indelibly — seared on my brain — a warning from the Beyond to remain true to the best that is in me though the heavens fall.

All the above is, of course, confidential. As so old and close a friend of his and ours I thought the facts would interest you.

My Mother is in fine health. His leaving her to untangle his chaotic affairs has proved to be the most merciful thing in the world. She has had no time to think or brood. And although this may sound strange to you, she is developing into a keenly interested business woman who seems to accept this unfamiliar responsibility with a great sense of relief. Under her hand, I honestly have a hunch that some dividends may finally accrue from the junk buried on the island of M.C.

Letter to George C. Tyler, 9 Dec. 1920

[The above was written four months after James O'Neill's death. Shaeffer, in *O'Neill: Son and Artist*, p. 39, says that James O'Neill's estate was valued at 'over one hundred and fifty thousand dollars'.]

I have been accused of unmitigated gloom. Is this a pessimistic view of life? I do not think so. There is a skin deep optimism and another higher optimism, not skin deep, which is usually confounded with pessimism. To me, the tragic alone has that significant beauty which is truth. It is the meaning of life — and the hope. The noblest is certainly the most tragic. The people who succeed and do not push on to a greater failure are the spiritual middle-classers. Their stopping at success is the proof of their compromising insignificance. How pretty their dreams must have been! The man who pursues the mere attainable should be sentenced to get it — and keep it. . . . Only through the unattainable does man achieve a hope worth living and dying for — and so attain himself. . . . [One] must state one's religion first in order not to be misunderstood, even if one makes no rash boast of always having the strength to live up to it. . . .

Letter to New York Tribune, 13 Feb. 1921,
defending Diff'rent, which had just opened

As soon as an author slips propaganda into a play everyone feels it and the play becomes simply an argument.

The Hairy Ape was propaganda in the sense that it was a symbol of man, who has lost his old harmony with nature, the harmony which he used to have as an animal and has not yet acquired in a spiritual way. Thus, not being able to find it on earth nor in heaven, he's in the middle, trying to make peace, taking the 'woist punches from bot' of 'em.' Yank can't go forward, and so he tries to go back. This is what his shaking hands with the gorilla meant. But he can't go back to 'belonging' either. The gorilla kills him. The subject here is the same ancient one that always was and always will be the one subject for drama, and that is man and his struggle with his own fate. The struggle used to be with the gods, but is now with himself, his own past, his attempt 'to belong'.

The most perfect plotless plays are those of Chekhov. But the newest thing now in playwriting is the opposite of the character play. It is the expressionistic play. For expressionism denies the value of characterization. As I understand it, expressionism tries to minimize everything on the stage that stands between the author and the audience. It strives to get the author talking directly to the audience. . . . The real contribution of the expressionist has been in the dynamic qualities of his plays. They express something in modern life better than did the old plays. I have something of this method in *The Hairy Ape*. But the character Yank remains a man and everyone recognizes him as such. . . .

I hardly ever go to the theatre, although I read all the plays I can get. I don't go to the theatre because I can always do a better production in my mind than the one on the stage. I have a better time and I am not bothered by the audience. No one sneezes during the scenes that interest me. Nor do I ever go to see one of my own plays — have seen only three of them since they started coming out. My real reason for this is that I was practically brought up in the theatre — in the wings — and I know all the technique of acting. I know everything that everyone is doing from the electrician to the stage hands. So I see the machinery going around all the time unless the play is wonderfully acted and produced. Then, too, in my own plays all the time I watch them I am acting all the parts and living them so intensely that by the time the performance is over I am exhausted — as if I had gone through a clothes wringer.

Interview in *New York Herald Tribune*, 16 Mar. 1924

I'll trust to Nietzsche for an interpretation as to what the Greeks thought of laughter. I agree with him even if he is wrong! . . .

I'm going in very heavily these days for the study of religion along certain definite lines I have mapped out as a sort of large background for certain work in the future I have in mind. Am also starting to study Ancient Greek which I never 'took' at college or prep. If in three or four years I'm able to read Greek tragedy in the original and enjoy it — the sound as well as the meaning — I'll have made a grand refuge for my soul to dive deeply and cooling into at moments when modern life — and drama — become too damn humid and shallow to be borne.

Letter to Manuel Komroff, 22 Mar. 1926.

A play form — return of my old idea of using structure of symphony or sonata — justification [of] my unconscious use of musical structure in nearly all of my plays — impulsion and chief interest always an attempt to do what music does (to express an essentially poetic view of life) using rhythms of recurrent themes — is my, at times, blunderingly vague groping and missing caused by just the very fact that my use of musical structure is unconscious and ignorant of its own laws? — feeling of great need now for fixed severe clearly apprehended form within which to create, now that I have finished breaking all realistic rules for modern drama — my adoption of archaic dramatic modes from Greek, Elizabethan — or ultra-modern Expressionistic or Strindbergian modes — not the answer because superficial does not strike at main deep-rooted impulse of creative ego toward self-expression in musical structure rhythm — when I attain clear knowledge and consciousness of such a structure as skeleton for all work will not my plays have real bone to them as well as flesh — up to now is not chief fault in plays that they lack bone in comparison to their superabundant flesh and meat — that their rickety bones are too frequently braced by splints carpentered in the dramatic technique surgery?

Notebook entry, Aug. 1931, printed in
Floyd, Eugene O'Neill at Work, p. 228-9

In *The Great God Brown* [1925] I would now [1932] make the masks symbolize more definitely the abstract theme of the play instead of, as in the old production, stressing the more superficial meaning that people wear masks before other people and are mistaken by them for their masks. . . .

With *Mourning Becomes Electra*, masks were called for in one draft of the three plays. But the classical connotation was too insistent. Masks in that connection demand great language to speak — which let me out of it with a sickening bump! So it evolved ultimately into the 'masklike faces' which expressed my intention tempered by the circumstances. . . .

'Second Thoughts', The American Spectator, Nov. 1932

[What] do I mean by an 'imaginative' theatre (where I hope for it, for example, in the subtitle of *Lazarus Laughed: a Play for an Imaginative*

Theatre)? I mean the one true theatre that could dare to boast — without committing a farcical sacrilege — that it is a legitimate descendant of the first theatre that sprang, by virtue of man's imaginative interpretation of life, out of his worship of Dionysos. I mean a theatre returned to its highest and sole significant function as a Temple where the religion of a poetical interpretation and symbolical celebration of life is communicated to human beings, starved in spirit by their soul-stifling daily struggle to exist as masks among the masks of the living! . . .

[Masks] would give [actors] the opportunity for a totally new kind of acting, that they would learn many undeveloped possibilities of their art if they appeared, even if only for a season or two, in masked roles.

'A Dramatist's Notebook,' *The American Spectator*, Jan. 1933

I'm going on the theory that the United States, instead of being the most successful country in the world, is the greatest failure. It's the greatest failure because it was given everything, more than any other country. Through moving as rapidly as it has, it hasn't acquired any real roots. Its main idea is that everlasting game of trying to possess your own soul by the possession of something outside it, thereby losing your own soul and the thing outside of it too.

America is the prime example of this because it happened so quickly and with such immense resources. This was really said in the Bible much better. We are the greatest example of 'For what shall it profit a man, if he gain the whole world and lose his own soul?' We had so much and could have gone either way.

Interview of 2 Sept. 1946, published in numerous periodicals, explaining the idea underlying the unfinished 'Cycle' of eleven 'American history' plays

a: Primary Sources

American Collected Editions

Particulars of first American editions of individual plays are included under play titles in Section 2.

Children of the Sea and Three Other Unpublished Plays by Eugene O'Neill, ed. Jennifer McCabe Atkinson (Washington, DC: NCR Microcard Editions, 1972).

Complete Plays 1913-1920, Complete Plays 1920-1931, Complete Plays 1932-1943, texts selected and notes by Travis Bogard (New York: Library of America, 1988).

Complete Works of Eugene O'Neill (New York: Boni and Liveright, 1924-25).

The Later Plays of Eugene O'Neill, ed. Travis Bogard (New York: Modern Library, 1967).

Lost Plays of Eugene O'Neill (New York: New Fathoms Press, 1950; reissued, New York: Citadel, 1963, and others).

Ten 'Lost' Plays of Eugene O'Neill, foreword by Bennett Cerf (New York: Random House, 1964).

The Plays of Eugene O'Neill, three volumes (New York: Random House, 1939, 1955).

Thirst and Other One-Act Plays (Boston: Gorham Press, 1914).

British Editions

The Collected Plays *have been published in London by Jonathan Cape (two vols., 1988). The following editions have also been published in London by Jonathan Cape:*

Plays: First Series: The Straw, The Emperor Jones, and Diff'rent (1922).

The Hairy Ape and Other Plays (1923) [also includes *Anna Cristie* and *The First Man*].

The Moon of the Caribees and Six Other Plays of the Sea (1923) [also includes *Bound East for Cardiff, The Long Voyage Home, In the Zone, Ile, Where the Cross Is Made*, and *The Rope*].

Beyond the Horizon (1924).

All God's Chillun Got Wings, Desire under the Elms, and *Welded* (1925).

The Great God Brown (1926) [also includes *The Fountain*, *The Dreamy Kid*, and *Before Breakfast*].
Marco Millions: a Play (1927).
Strange Interlude: a Play (1928).
Lazarus Laughed and Dynamo: Two Plays (1929).
Mourning Becomes Electra: a Trilogy (1932).
Ah, Wilderness! and Days Without End: Two Plays (1934).
The Iceman Cometh (1947).
A Moon for the Misbegotten: a Play in Four Acts (1953).
Long Day's Journey into Night (1956).
A Touch of the Poet: a Play in Four Acts (1957).
Hughie: a Play (1962).
More Stately Mansions: a Play in Three Acts (1965).

Miscellaneous Writings

Bogard, Travis, and Jackson Bryer, eds., *Selected Letters of Eugene O'Neill* (New Haven: Yale University Press, 1988).

Bryer, Jackson R., with Ruth M. Alvarez, eds., introductory essays by Travis Bogard, *The Theatre We Worked For* (New Haven and London: Yale Univ. Press, 1981). [Correspondence with Kenneth Macgowan.]

The Calms of Capricorn: a Play Developed from O'Neill's Scenario by Donald Gallup with a Transcription of the Scenario (New Haven and New York: Ticknor and Fields, 1982).

Chris Christophersen, foreword by Leslie Eric Comens (New York: Random House, 1982).

Commins, Dorothy, ed., *Love and Admiration and Respect*, foreword by Travis Bogard (Durham, NC: Duke University Press, 1986). [Correspondence with Saxe Commins.]

Estrin, Mark W., ed., *Conversations with Eugene O'Neill* (Jackson and London: University of Mississippi Press, 1990).

Floyd, Virginia, ed., *Eugene O'Neill at Work: Newly Released Ideas for Plays* (New York: Ungar, 1981).

Floyd, Virginia, ed., *Eugene O'Neill: the Unfinished Plays* (New York: Ungar, 1988).

Gallup, Donald, ed., *Eugene O'Neill: Work Diaries*, two vols. (New Haven: Yale University Library, 1981).

Gallup, Donald, ed., *Eugene O'Neill's Poems 1912-1944* (New Haven and New York: Ticknor and Fields, 1980).

Roberts, Nancy L., and Arthur W. Roberts, eds., *As Ever, Gene* (Rutherford, London, and Toronto: Fairleigh Dickinson University Press, 1987). [Correspondence with George Jean Nathan.]

b: Secondary Sources

Criticism and Biography

Barlow, Judith, *Final Acts: the Creation of Three Late O'Neill Plays* (Athens, GA: University of Georgia Press, 1985). [Valuable study of the evolution of the late plays, based on study of the manuscripts.]

Basso, Hamilton, 'The Tragic Sense', *New Yorker*, 28 Feb., 6 Mar., 13 Mar. 1948. {Factually unreliable, but interesting for the author's impressions of his meetings with O'Neill.]

Black, Stephen A., 'Eugene O'Neill in Mourning', Biography XI, 1 (Winter 1988), p. 16-34.

Bogard, Travis, *Contours in Time: the Plays of Eugene O'Neill* (New York: Oxford University Press, 1972). [The life and work.]

Boulton, Agnes, *Part of a Long Story* (Garden City, NY: Doubleday, 1958). [Interesting memoir by O'Neill's second wife.]

Bowen, Croswell, assisted by Shane O'Neill, *Curse of the Misbegotten: a Tale of the House of O'Neill* (New York: McGraw-Hill, 1959). [Breezy but occasionally interesting for the contributions of O'Neill's second son.]

Cargill, Oscar, N. B. Fagin, and W. J. Fisher, eds., *O'Neill and His Plays: Four Decades of Criticism* (New York: New York University Press, 1961).

Carpenter, Frederick, *Eugene O'Neill*, revised ed. (Boston: Twayne, 1979).

Chabrowe, Leonard, *Ritual and Pathos: the Theater of Eugene O'Neill* (Lewisburg, Pa: Bucknell University Press, 1976).

Chothia, Jean, *Forging a Language: a Study of the Plays of Eugene O'Neill* (Cambridge: Cambridge University Press, 1979).

Floyd, Virginia, ed., *Eugene O'Neill: a World View* (New York: Ungar, 1979). [Articles and reminiscences.]

Frenz, Horst and Susan Tuck, *Eugene O'Neill's Critics: Voices from Abroad* (Carbondale: Southern Ilinois University Press, 1984).

Gassner, John, ed., *O'Neill: a Collection of Critical Essays* (Englewood Cliffs, NJ: Prentice-Hall, 1964).

Gelb, Arthur, and Barbara, *O'Neill* (New York: Harper and Row, 1962; enlarged ed. 1973). [First authoritative biography.]

Manheim, Michael, *Eugene O'Neill's New Language of Kinship* (Syracuse, NY: Syracuse University Press, 1982). [A psycho-analytically informed study of the relation of O'Neill's life to the plays.]

Martine, James J., *Critical Essays on Eugene O'Neill* (Boston: G. K. Hall, 1984).

Miller, Jordan Y., ed., *Playwright's Progress: O'Neill and the Critics* (Chicago: Scott, Foresman, 1965).

Quintero, Jose, *If You Don't Dance They Beat You* (Boston: Little, Brown, 1974). [Memoir of the noted director.]

Raleigh, John Henry, *The Plays of Eugene O'Neill* (Carbondale: Southern Illinois University Press, 1965).

Raleigh, John Henry, ed. *Twentieth Century Interpretations of The Iceman Cometh: a Collection of Critical Essays* (Englewood Cliffs, NJ: Prentice-Hall, 1968).

Ranald, Margaret Loftus, *The Eugene O'Neill Companion* (Westport, Conn: Greenwood Press, 1984). [Useful and reliable.]

Reaver, J. Russell, *An O'Neill Concordance*, three vols. (Detroit: Gale Research Press, 1969).

Robinson, James, *Eugene O'Neill and Oriental Thought* (Carbondale: Southern Illinois University Press, 1982).

Shaughnessy, Edward L., *Eugene O'Neill in Ireland: the Critical Reception* (New York and London: Greenwood Press, 1988).

Sheaffer, Louis, *O'Neill, Son and Playwright* (Boston: Little, Brown, 1968). [O'Neill's life to 1920.]

Sheaffer, Louis, *O'Neill, Son and Artist* (Boston: Little, Brown, 1973). [Completes the foregoing, an admirable biography.]

Tiusanen, Timo, *O'Neill's Scenic Images* (Princeton: Princeton University Press, 1968).

Tornqvist, Egil, *A Drama of Souls: Studies in O'Neill's Super-Naturalistic Technique* (Uppsala: Universitatis Upsaliensis, 1968).

Vena, Gary, *O'Neill's The Iceman Cometh: Reconstructing the Premiere* (Ann Arbor and London: UMI Research, 1988).

Wainscott, Ronald H., *Staging O'Neill: the Experimental Years 1920-1934* (New Haven and London: Yale University Press, 1988).

Journals

The Eugene O'Neill Newsletter, triannual, Vols. I-XII (1977-1988), succeeded by *The Eugene O'Neill Review*, biannual, commencing as Vol. XIII (1989, in progress). Edited by Frederick C. Wilkins. An indispensable source of current scholarship, as well as information on bibliographical and performance matters.]

Bibliography

Atkinson, Jennifer McCabe, *Eugene O'Neill: a Descriptive Bibliography* (Pittsburg: University of Pittsburg, 1974). [Indispensable; includes reproductions of covers and title pages.]

Bryer, Jackson R., *Checklist of Eugene O'Neill* (Columbus, Ohio: Charles F. Merrill, 1971).

Frenz, Horst. 'A List of Foreign Editions and Translations of Eugene O'Neill's Dramas', *Bulletin of Bibliography*, XVIII (1943), p. 33-4.

Miller, Jordan Y., *Eugene O'Neill and the American Critic: a Bibliographic Checklist*, second ed. (Hamden, Conn.: Archon, 1973).

Smith, Madeline, and Richard Eaton, *Eugene O'Neill: an Annotated Bibliography* (New York and London: Garland, 1988). [Supplements Miller's work, above.]